MW00437906

WHY YOUR DOG THINKS YOU'RE A HERO

I WUFF YOU

the hilarious
guide to all
the reasons
your dog thinks
you're the best

SAM HART

ILLUSTRATED BY **FIN KENDALL**

summersdale

CONGRATULATIONS, YOU'VE MADE ONE OF LIFE'S MOST IMPORTANT DECISIONS:

YOU'VE REALIZED YOU'RE A DOG PERSON!

Not only have you gained a best friend and a second shadow, but you've also found the president of your very own fan club. And what do you do to deserve such an honour? Little more than get out of bed in the morning, arrive home after work, and say the word "walkies".

They might be easily pleased, but we think they have the very best attitude – especially when it comes to cheering on their owners.

But please, don't just take our word for it – let your dog explain the many different reasons why they think you're an absolute hero!

Humans are so clever – they can put on their own leads without any help!

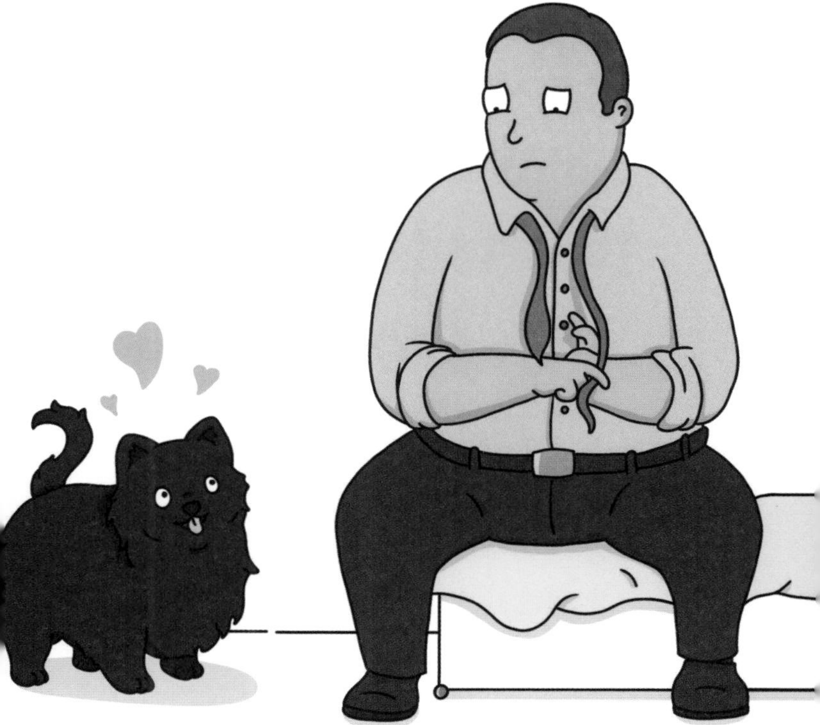

Our families leave out new toys for us every day. They're so thoughtful!

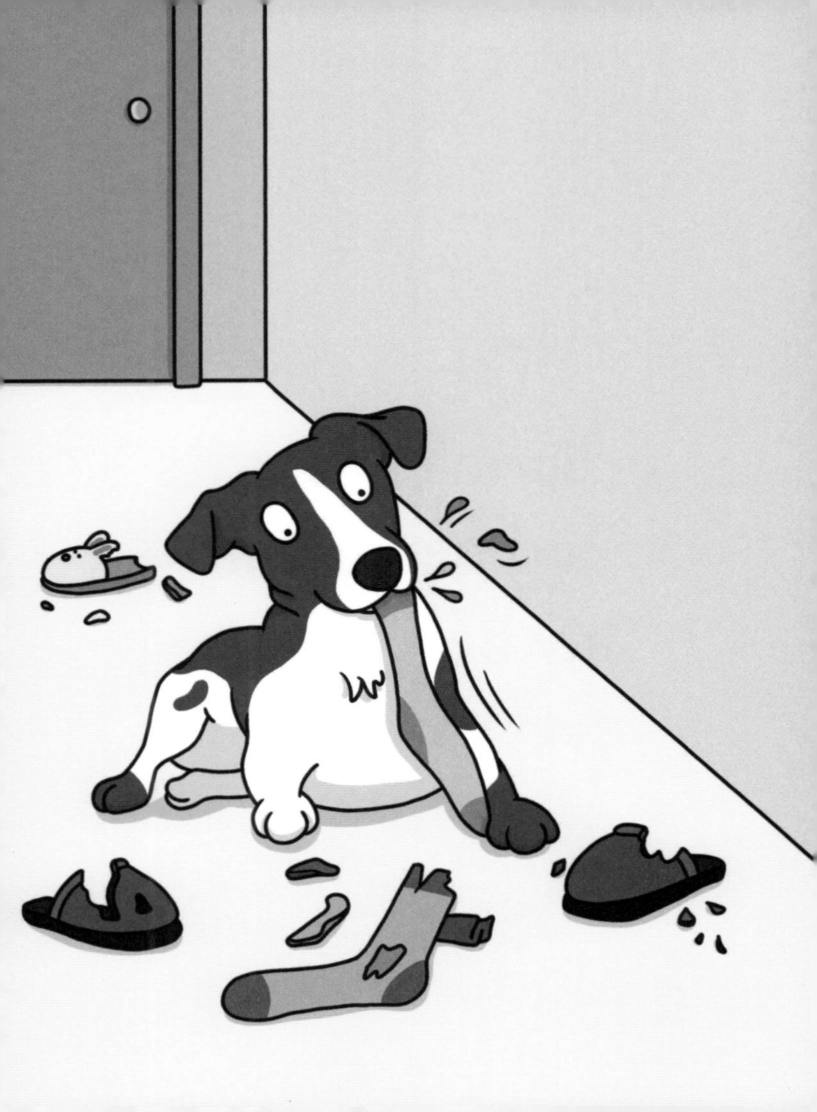

They keep
ordering presents
so I get to see
my best friend
every morning!

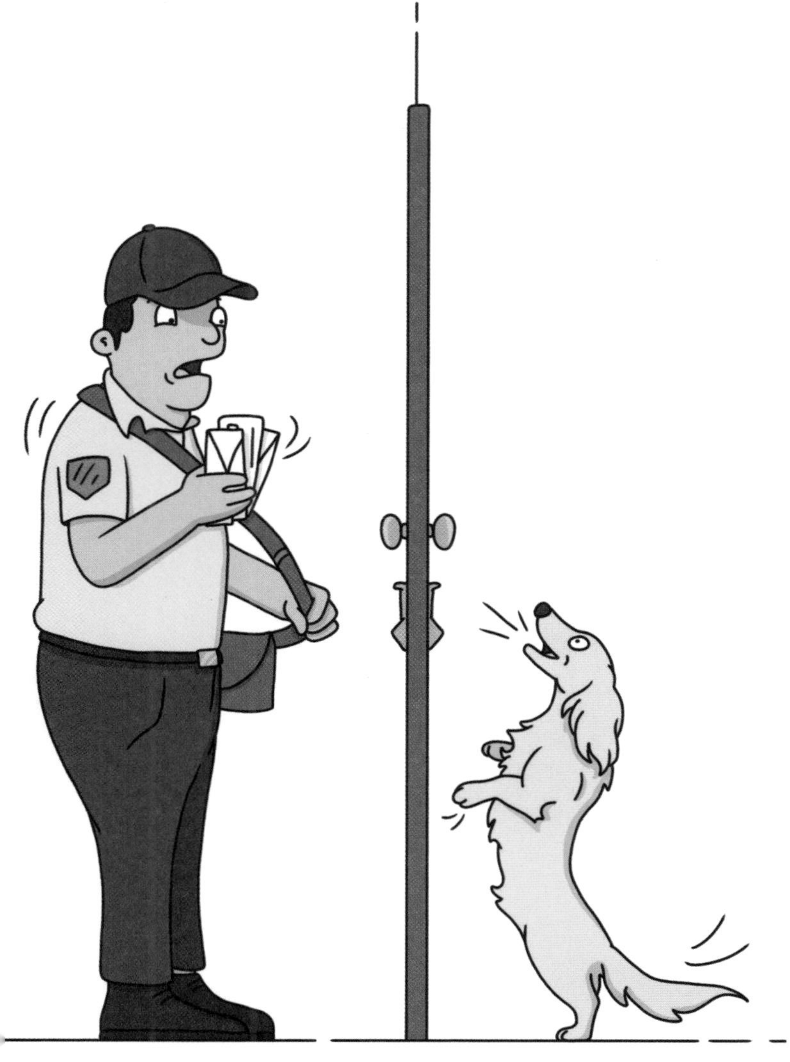

There's always
room for us
on their lap!

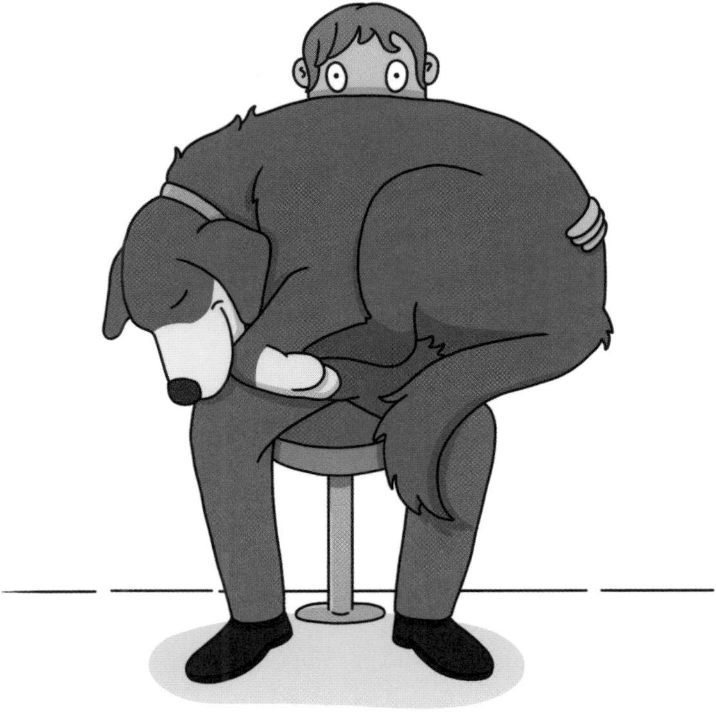

Our owners are so supportive – they cheer us on so we can run even faster!

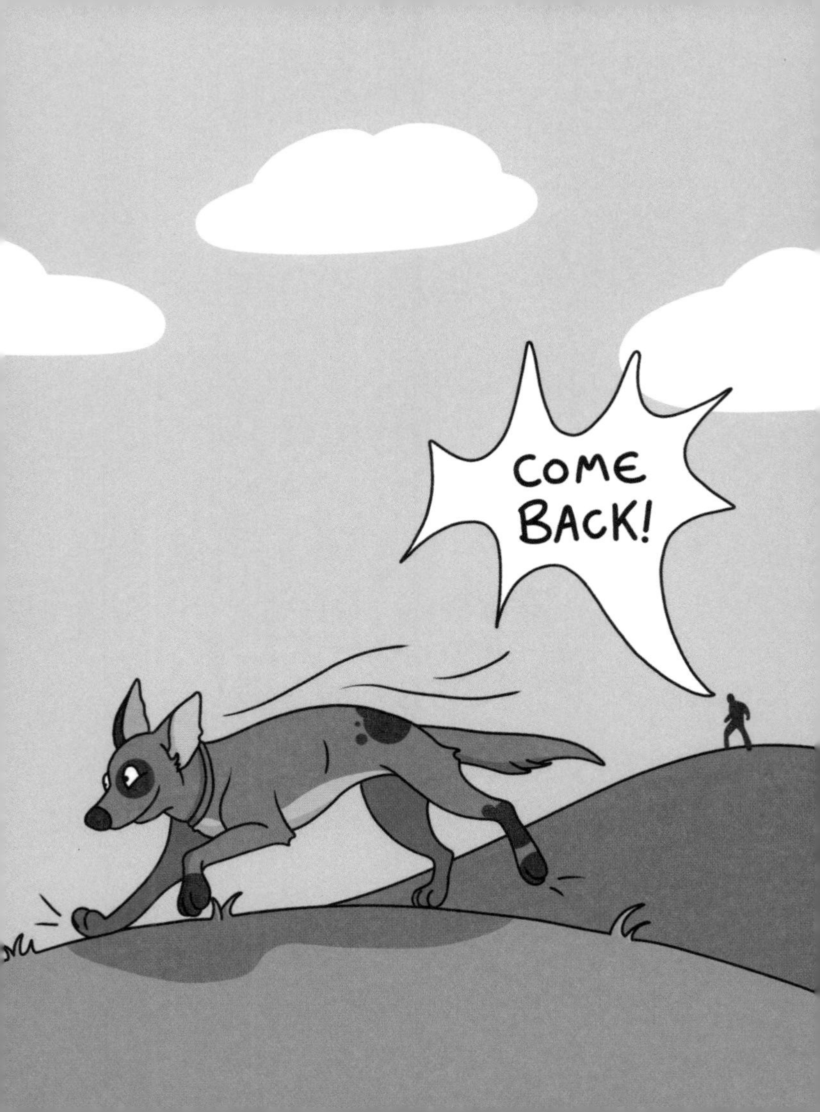
COME BACK!

Even when it rains, they still love a long, bracing walk!

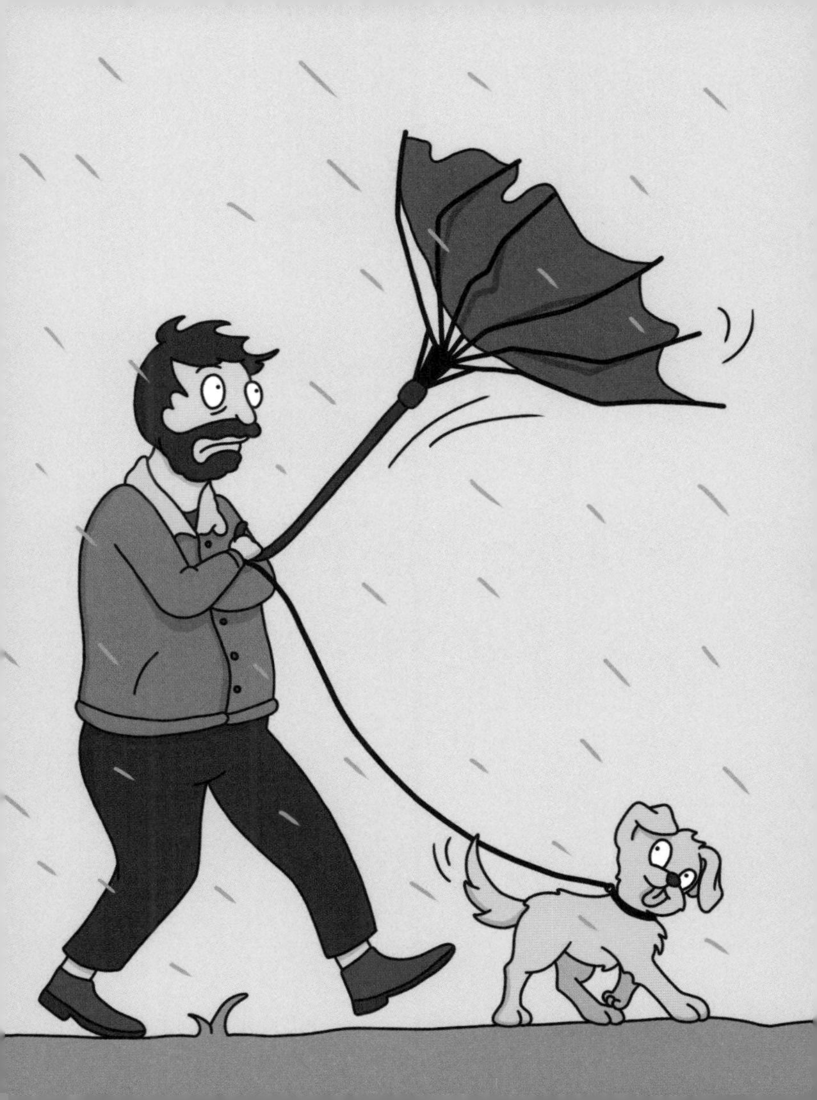

Humans are
so gracious – they
even taste-test
our second
dinners!

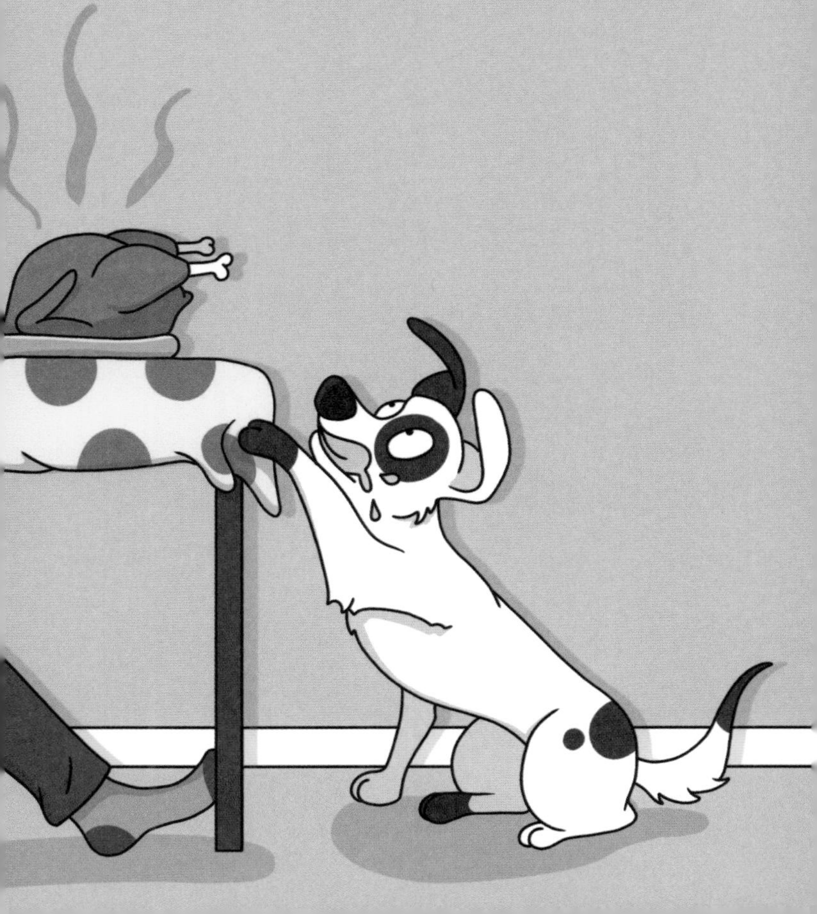

You know it's love when they keep little bags of your poop.

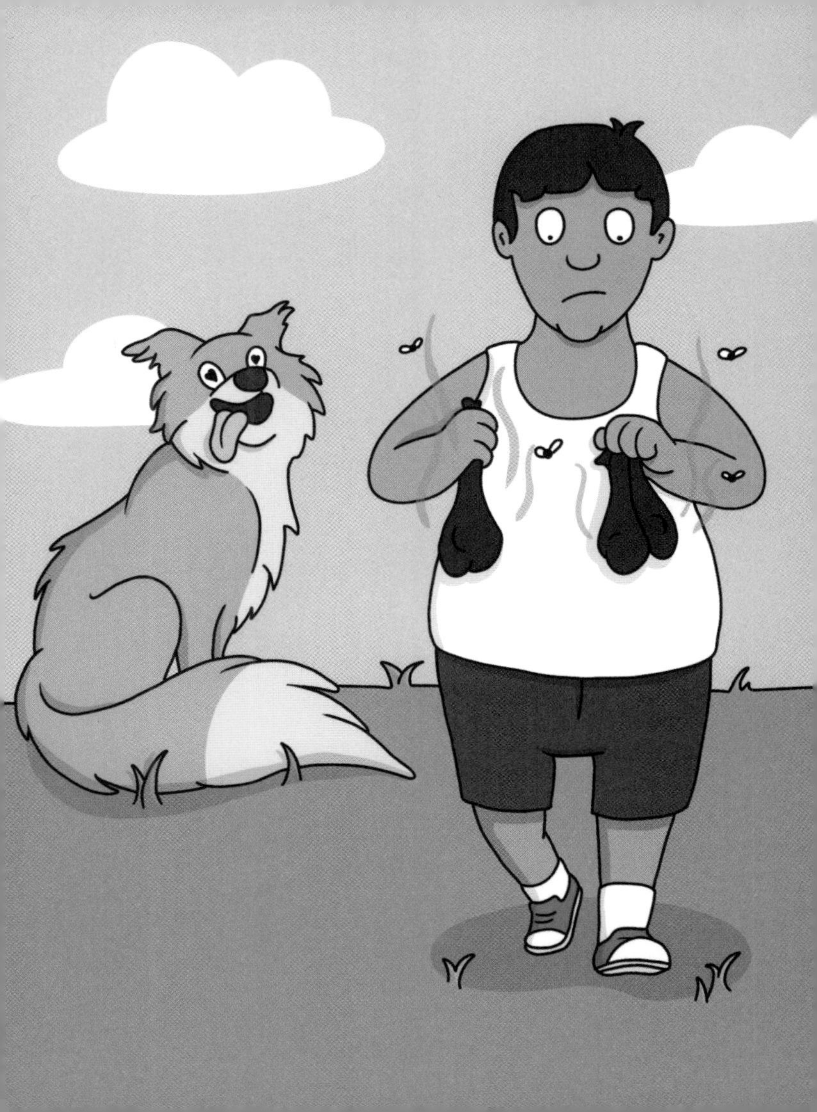

They never get tired of playing ball with us!

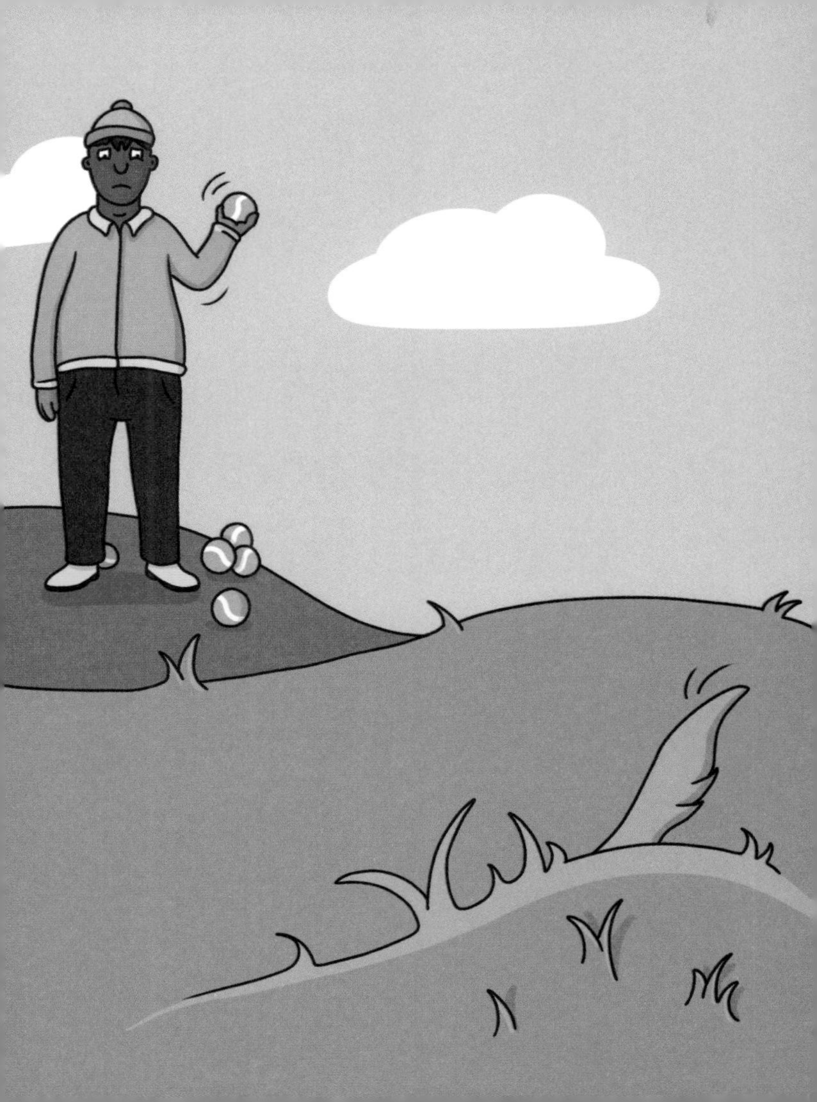

They are
the only ones
that can defeat
the evil, noisy
dust-machine.

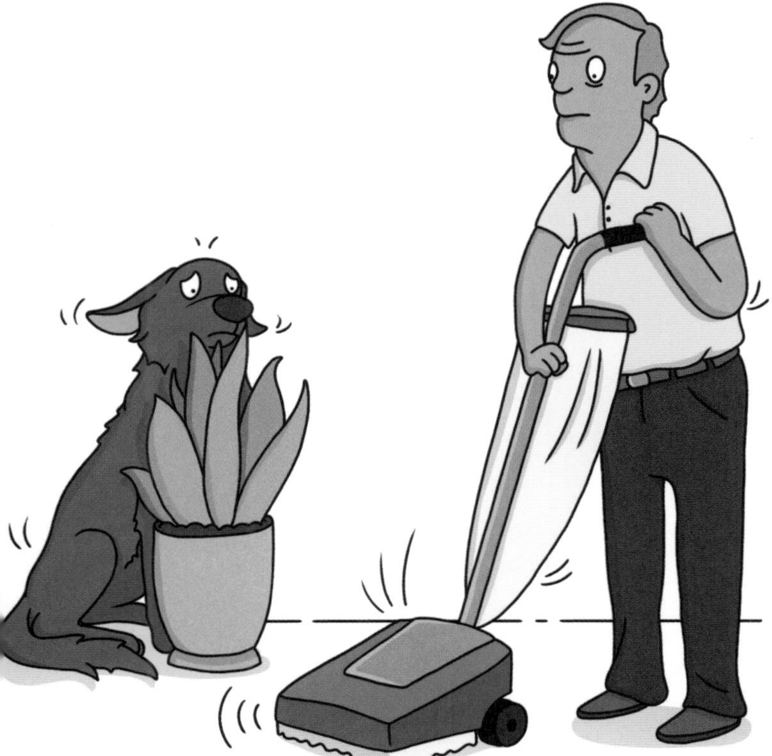

They love public
displays of
affection even
more than we do!

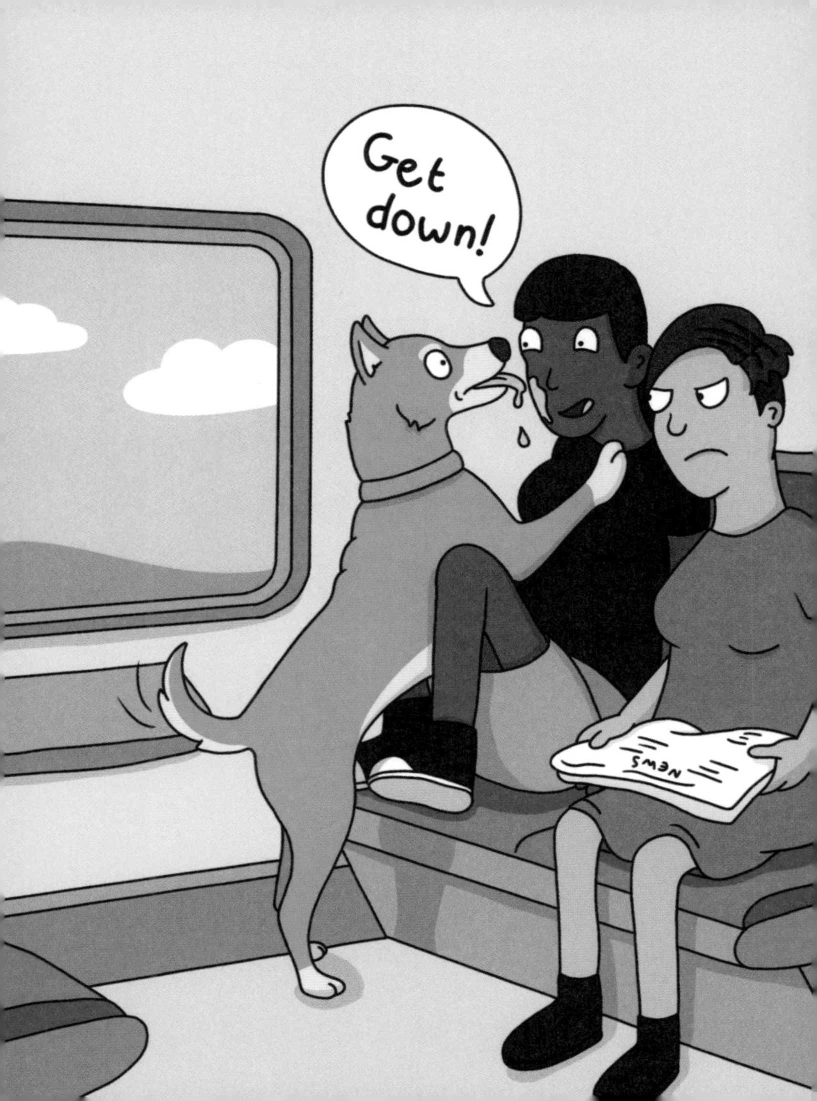
Get down!

Every now and
then humans
treat us to a
little me-time.

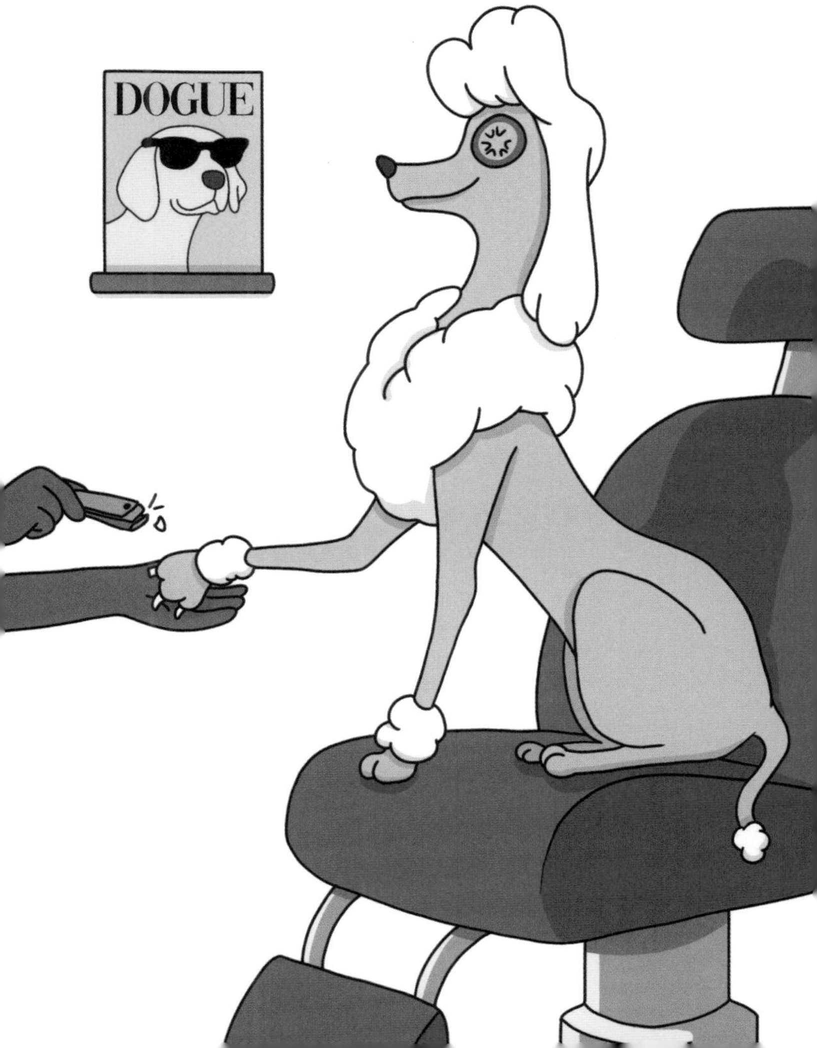
DOGUE

They love
a treasure hunt
just as much
as we do!

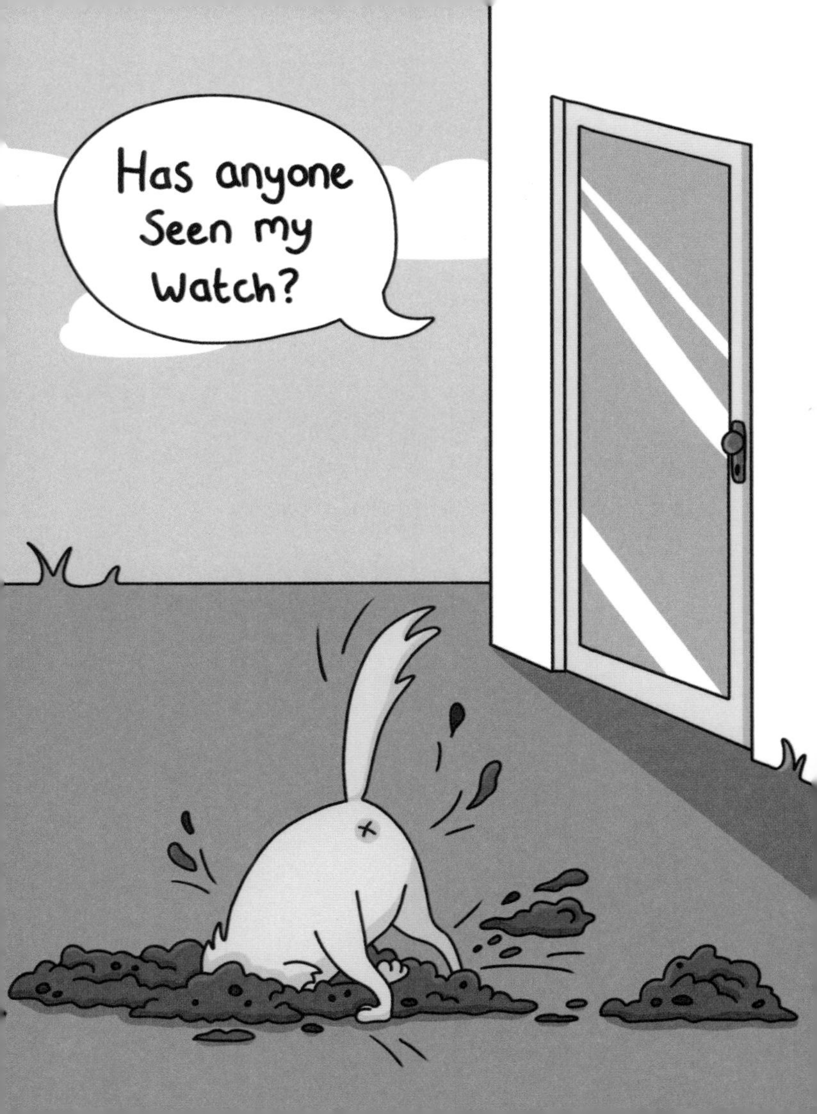
Has anyone Seen my Watch?

They love our company, no matter what time of day it is.

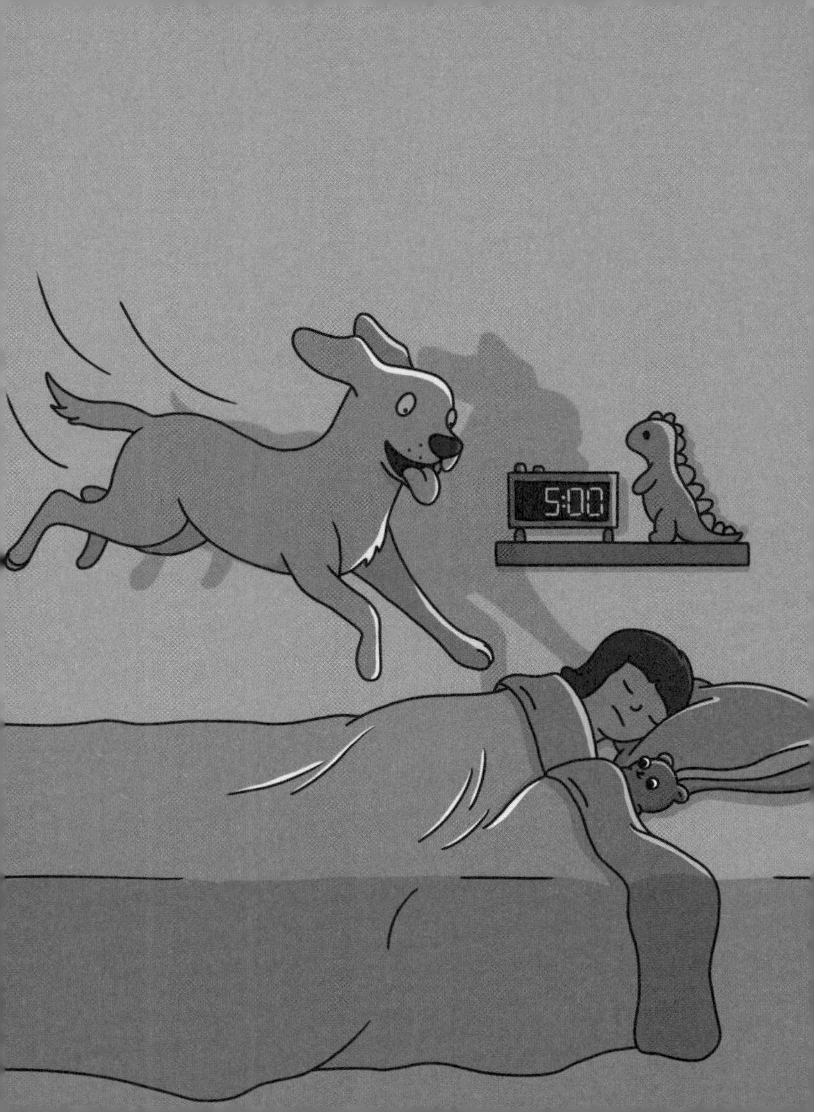
5:00

They are the
best at finding
our lost toys!

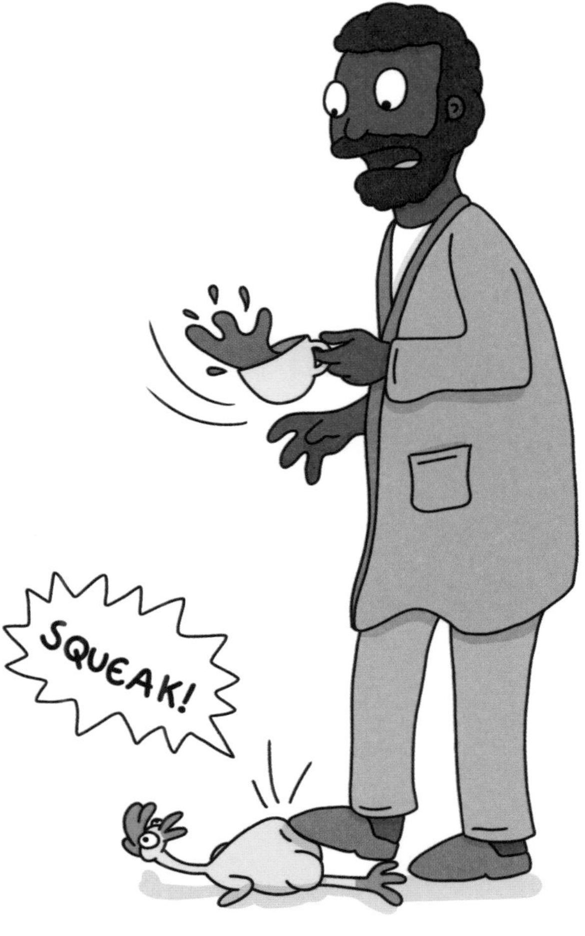
SQUEAK!

Even the littlest ones know how to have fun!

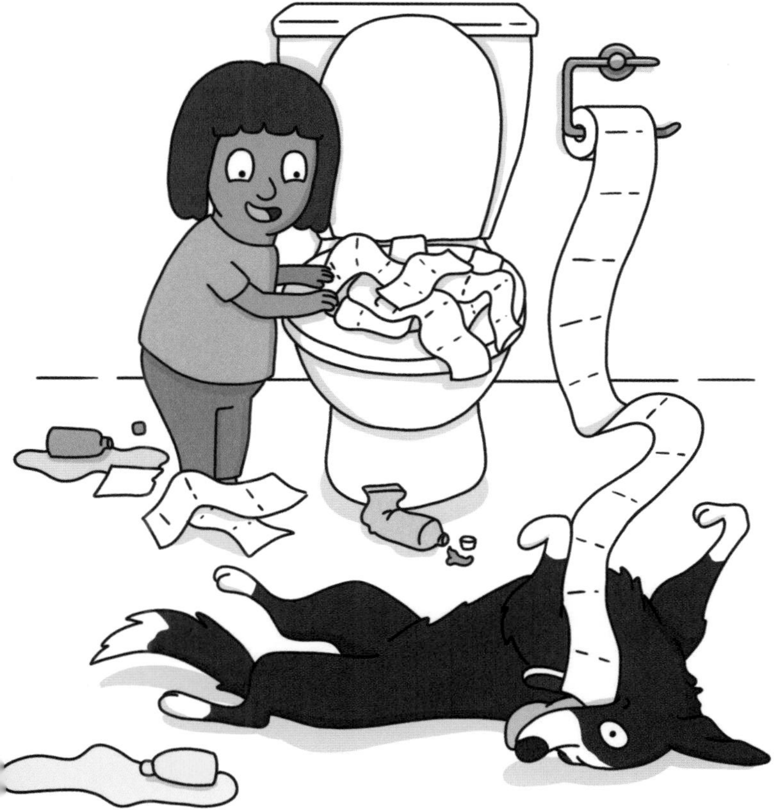

Their
resourcefulness
knows no bounds!

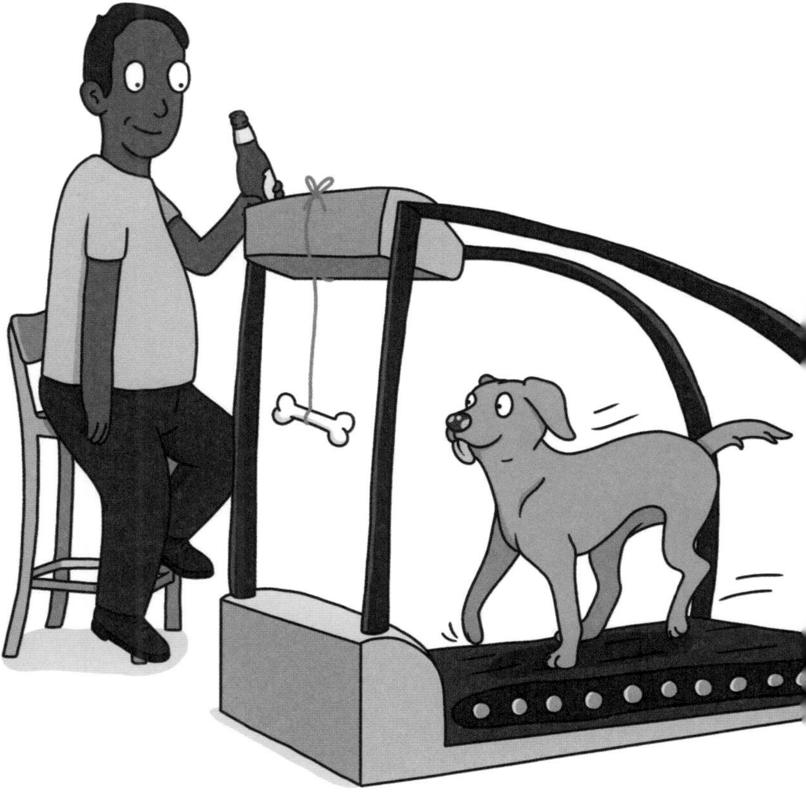

They make sure we're never left out during special times of the year!

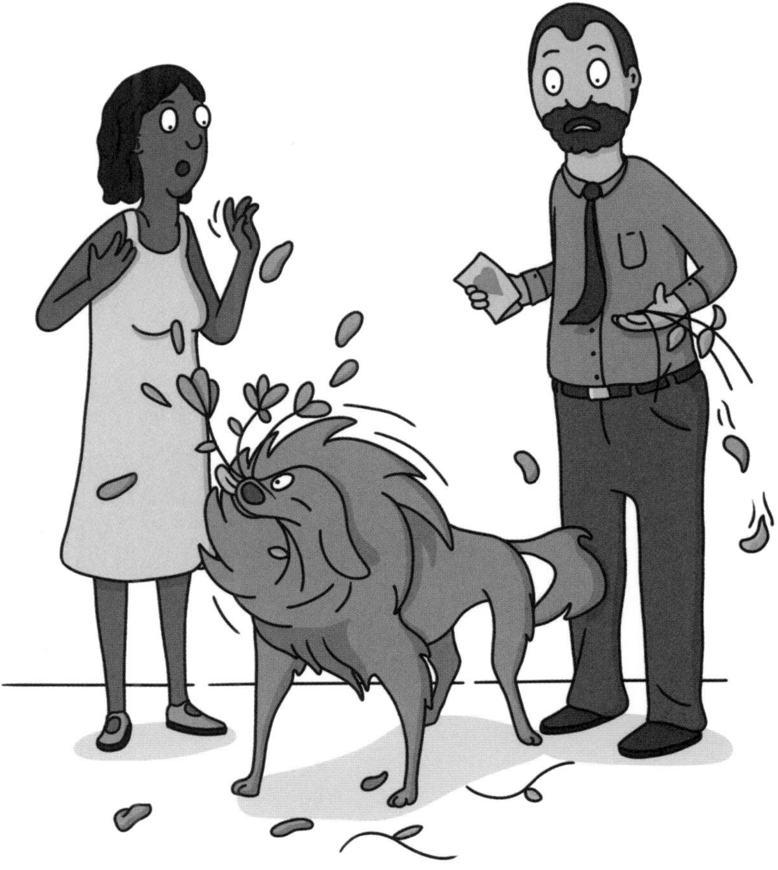

Our walks always include the best snacks!

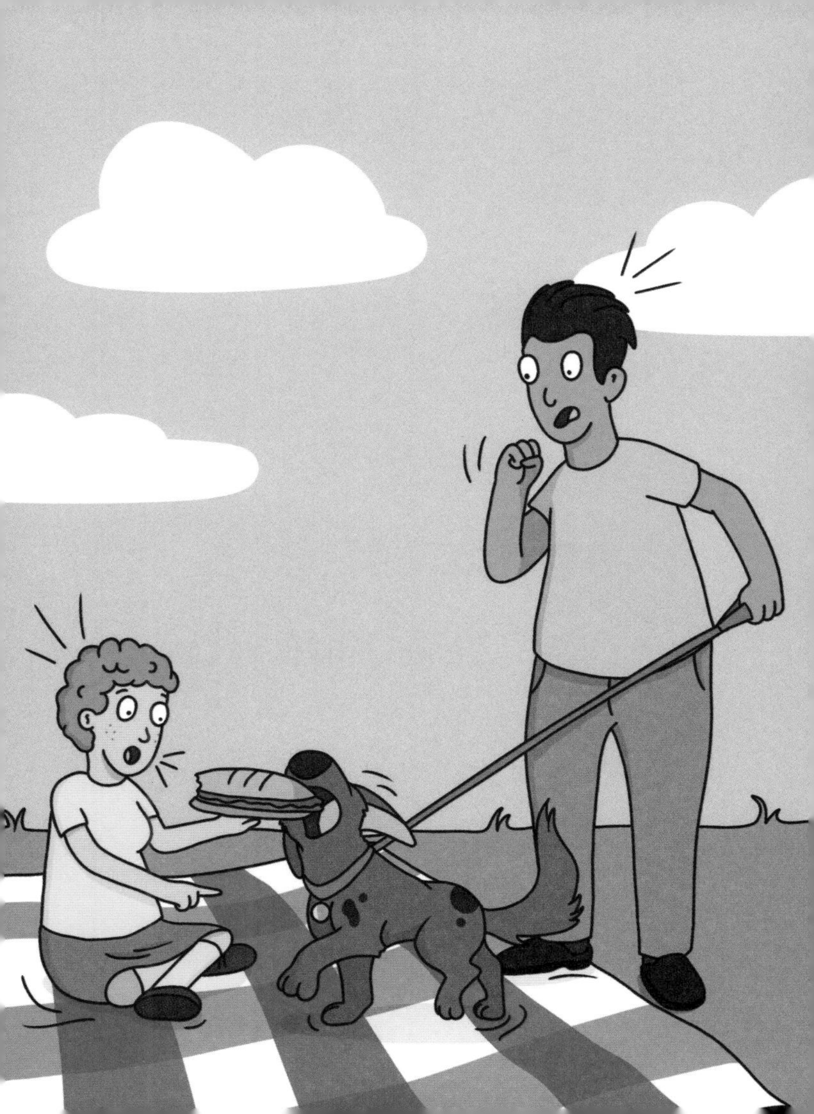

Our quest for the perfect stick is their top priority.

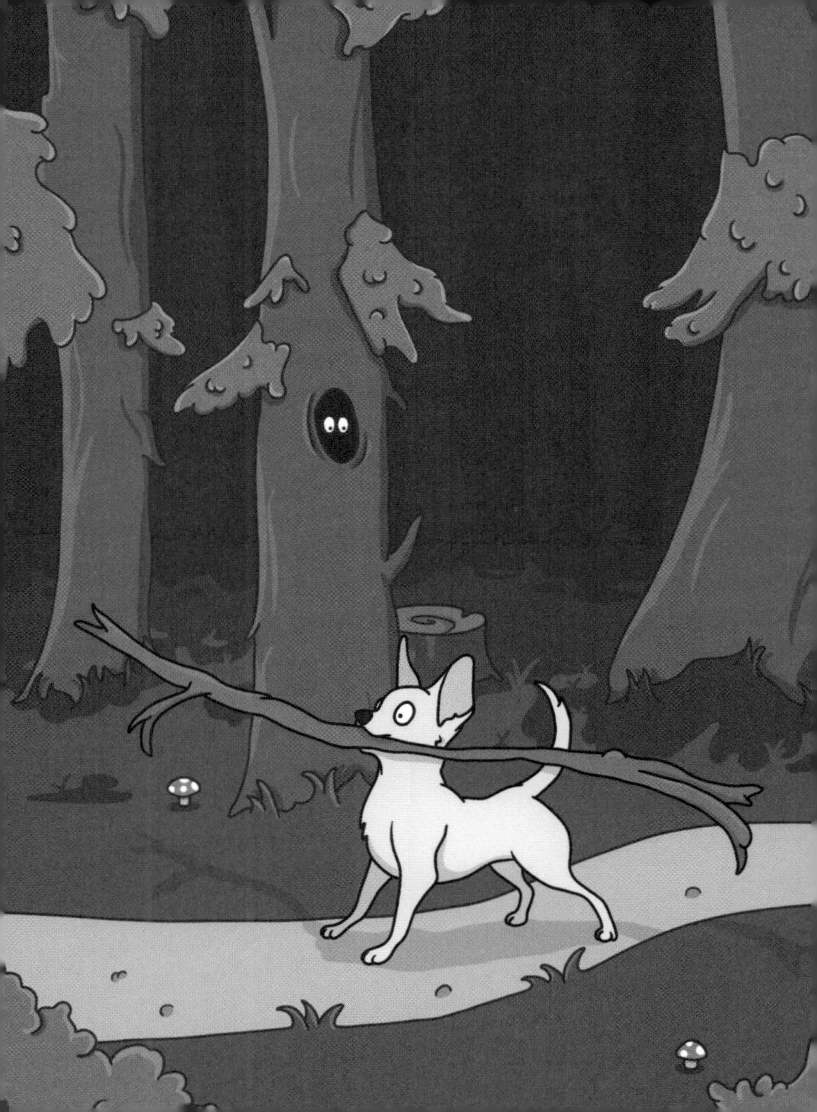

Humans share
our guard duties
so we get to
relax when it's
their turn to
keep watch.

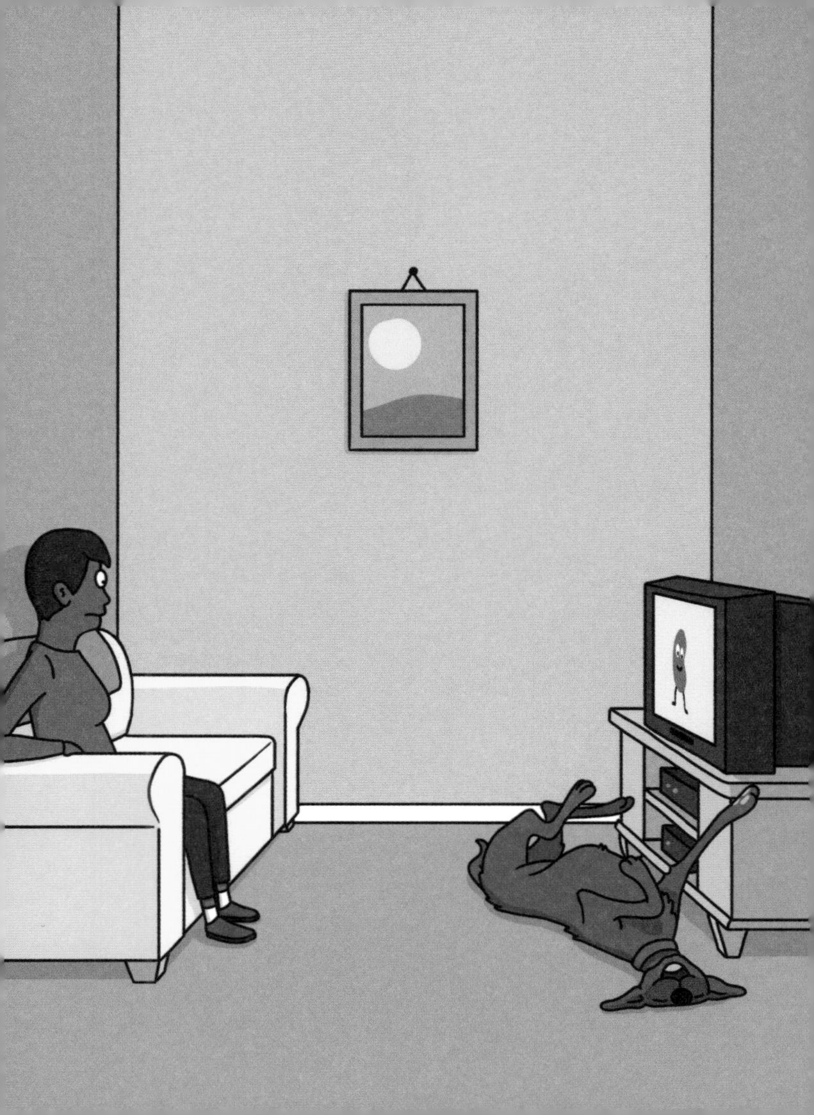

We love it when
we get to give
each other a bath!

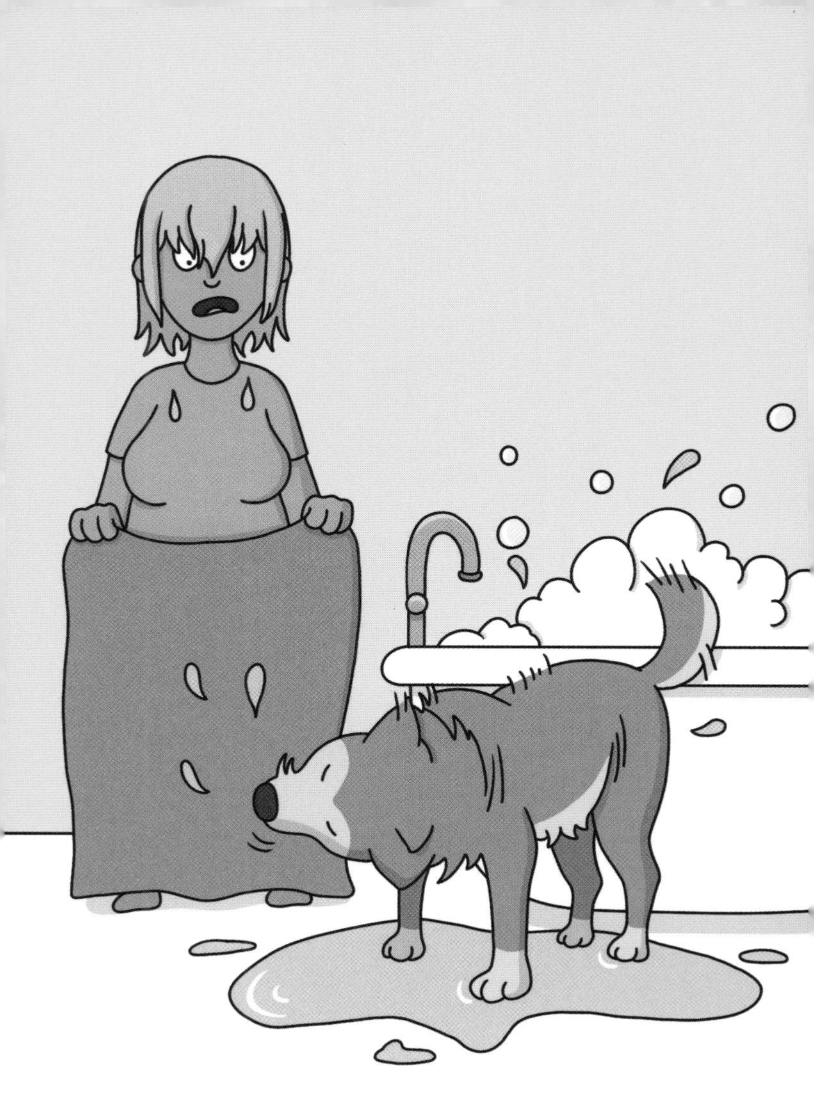

They are always keen to play tug of war with us.

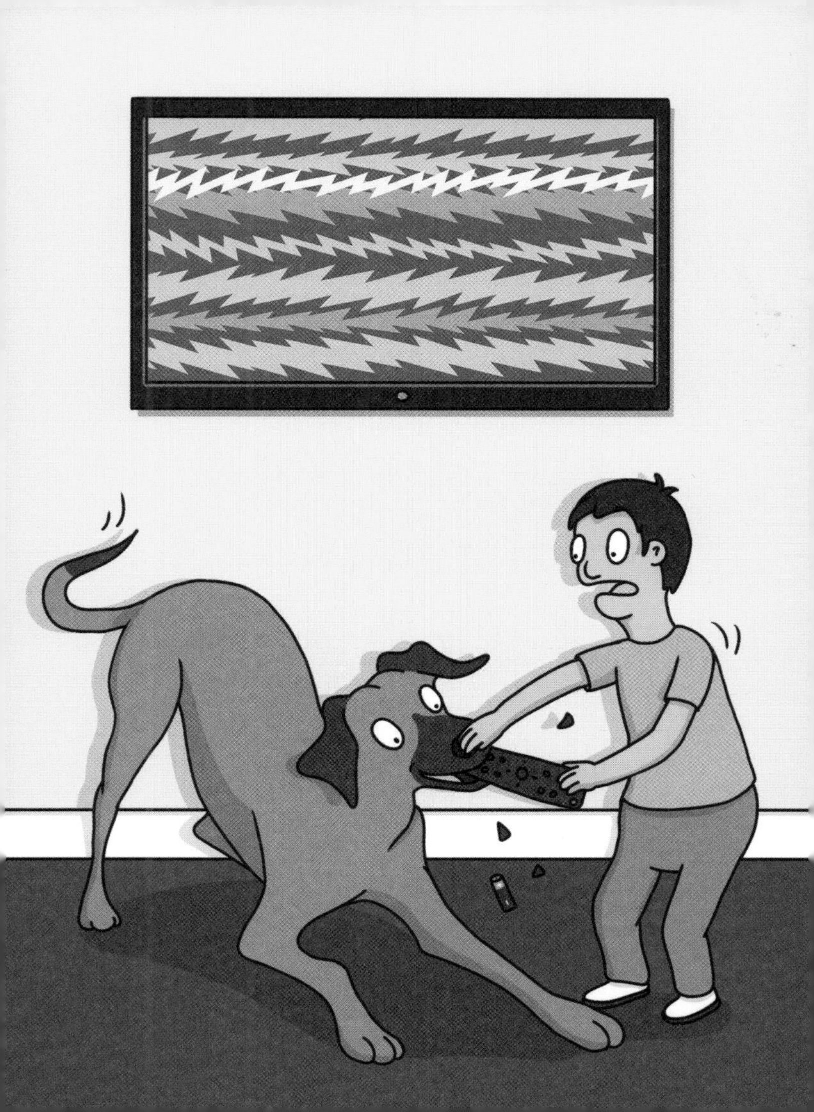

They let us go out
on the town with
all our friends!

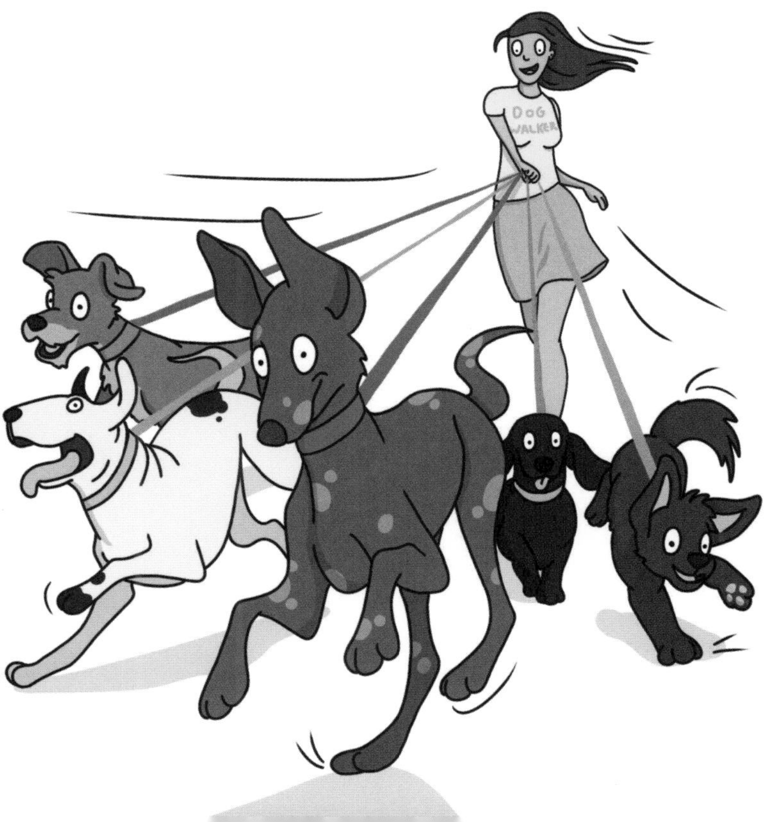
DOG
WALKER

They invest in
our education.

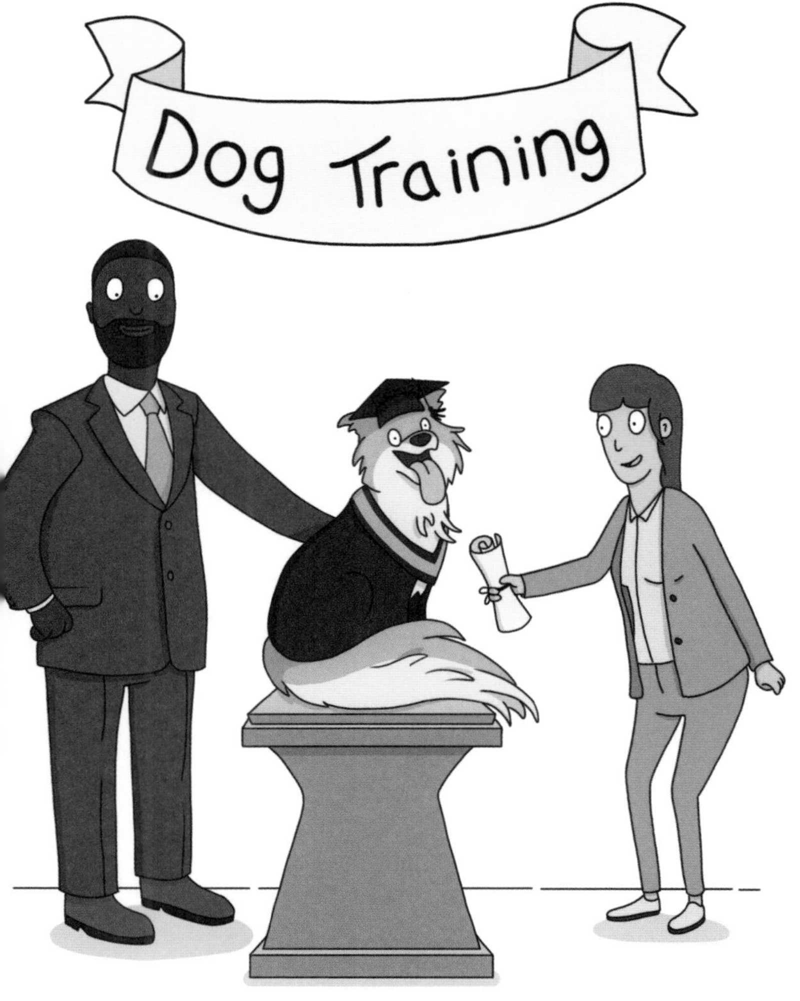
Dog Training

They know that exercise is more fun when you do it together!

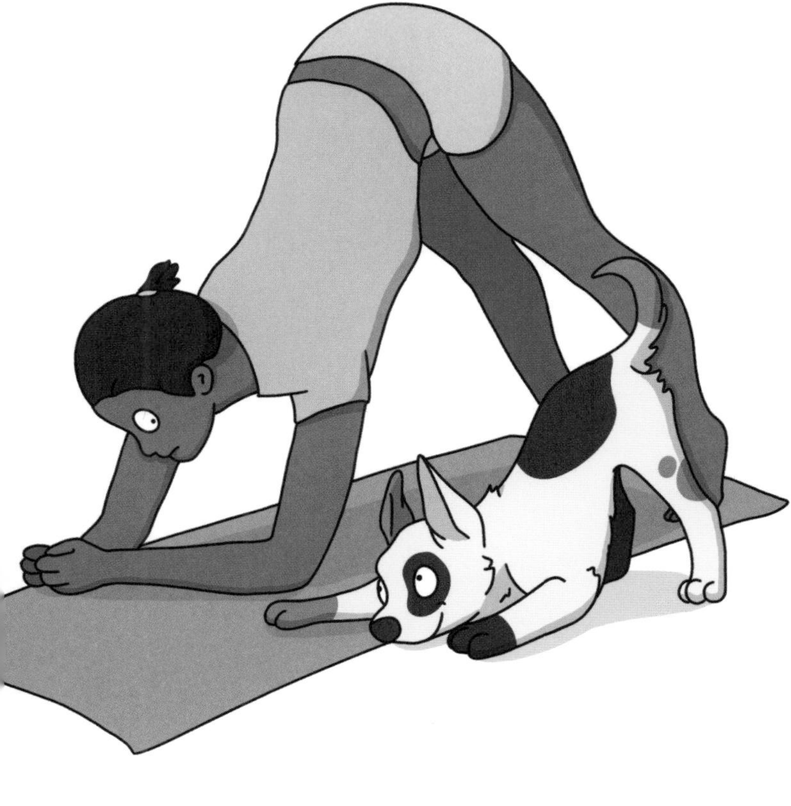

They support us
in our mission to
make friends with
the squirrels!

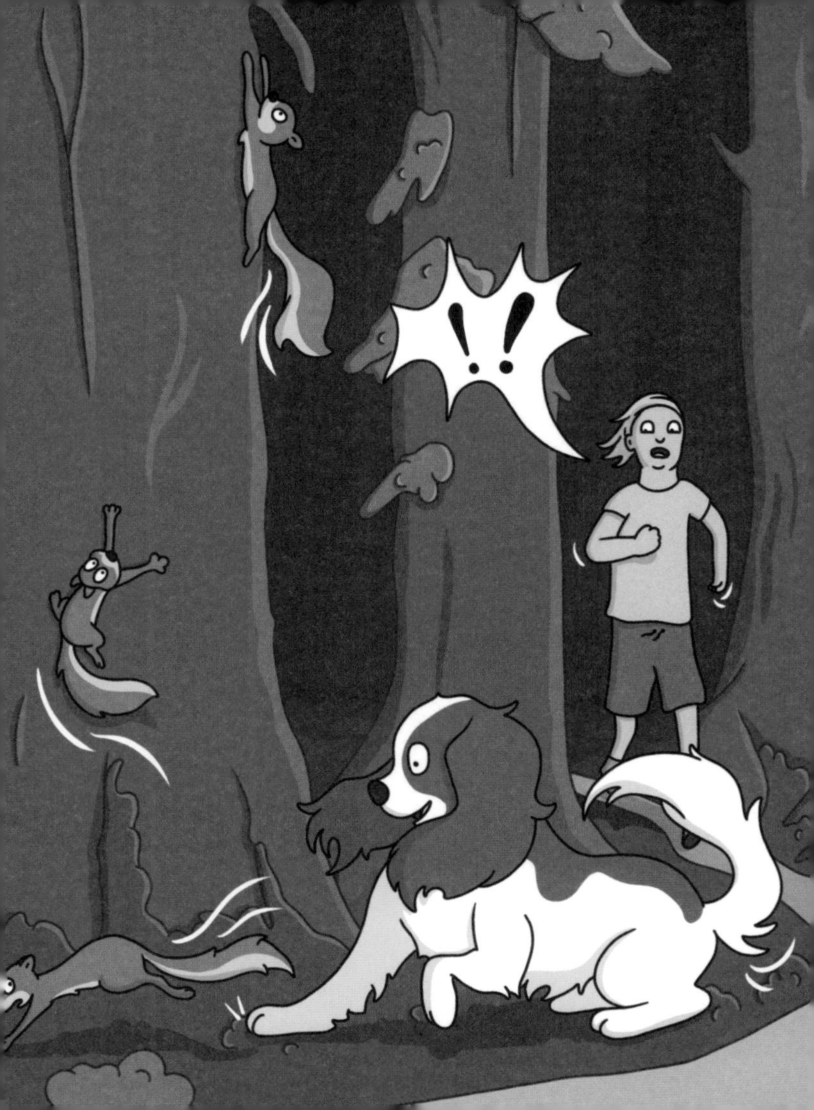
!!

We love it
when they help
us reinvent
ourselves!

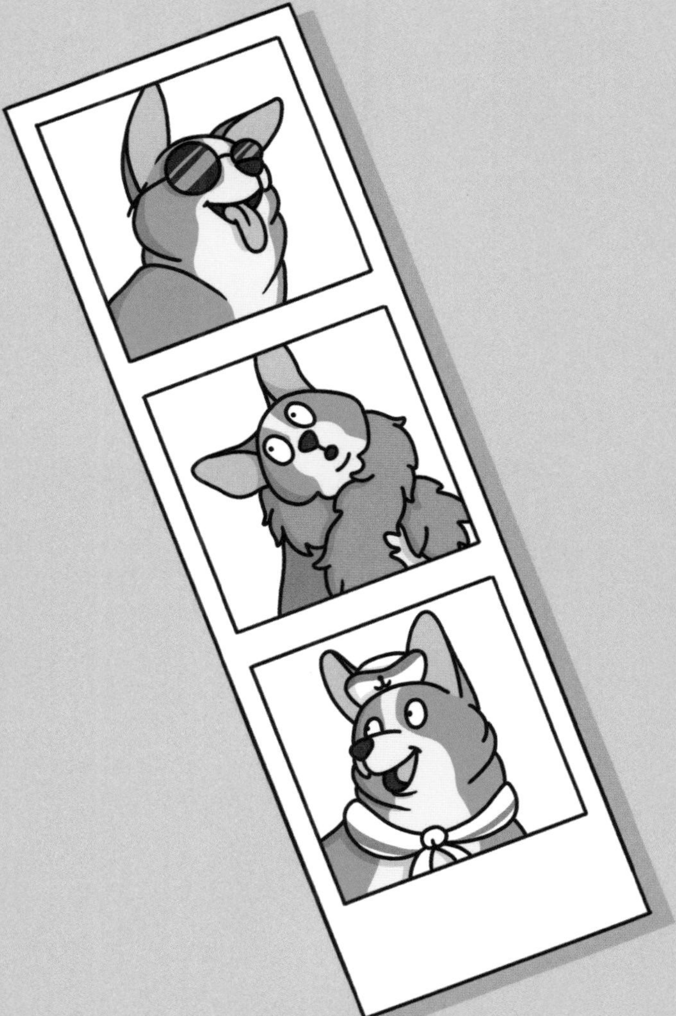

Thanks to them,
we can now spell.

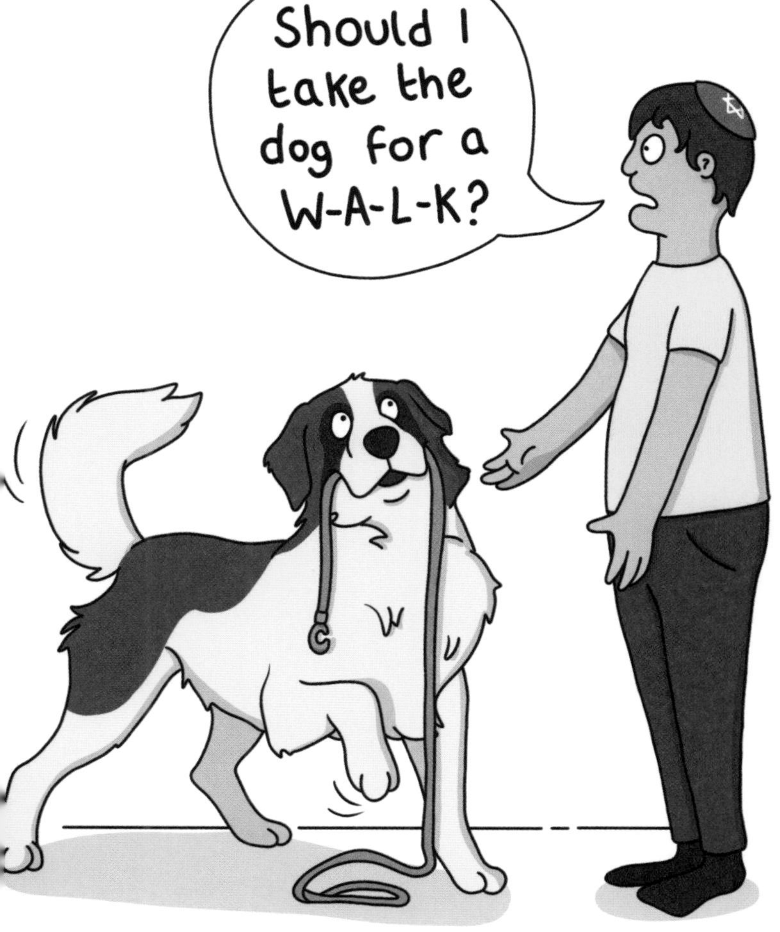
Should I take the dog for a W-A-L-K?

They let us call
shotgun on every
single road trip!

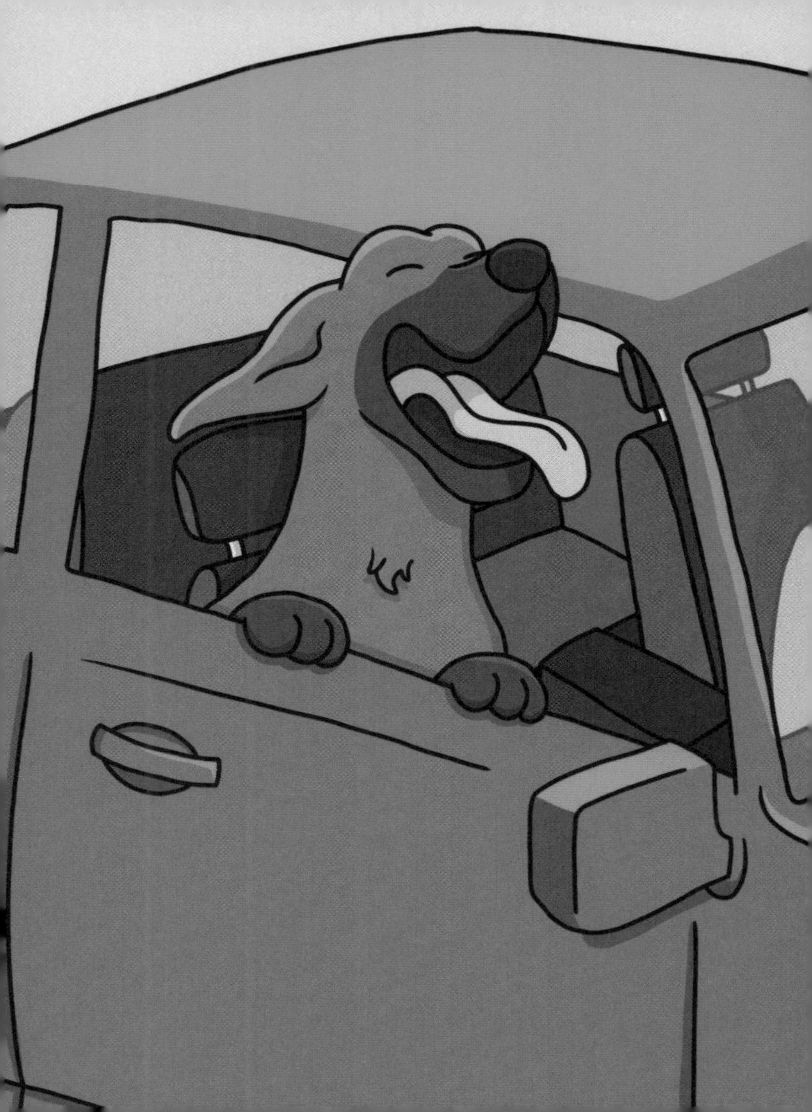

Sometimes we get to go to the beach to do some landscaping!

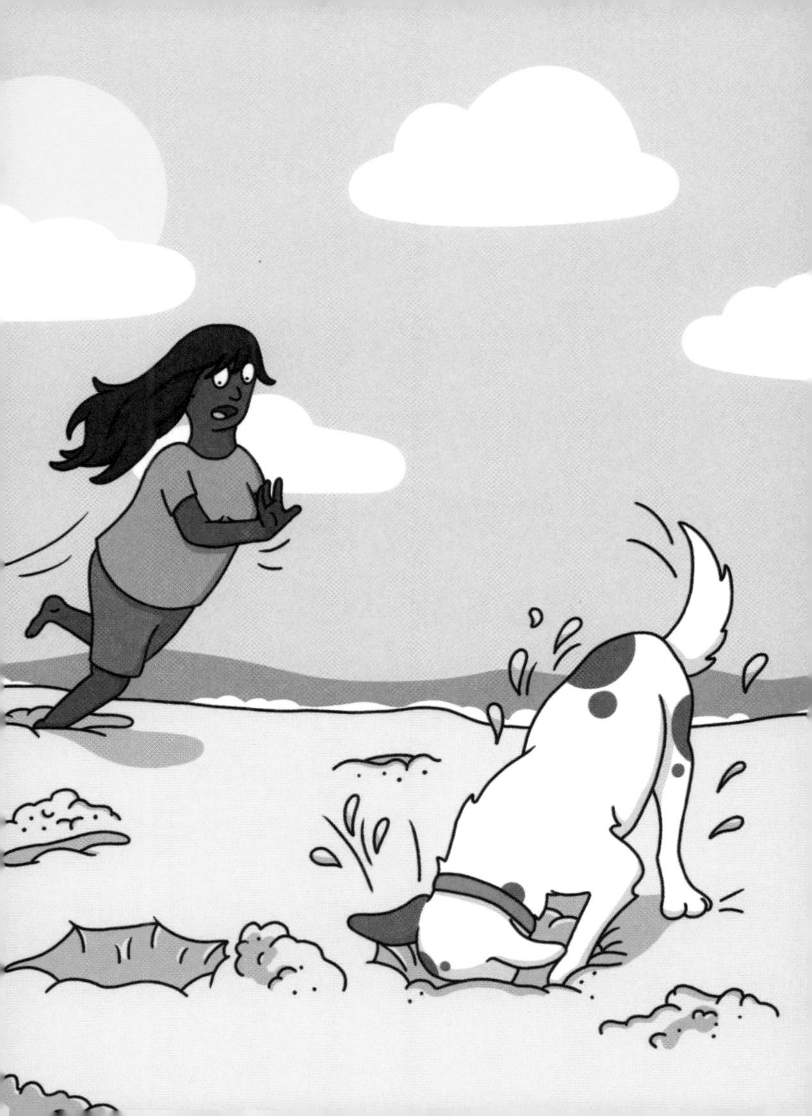

They escort us
to our important
meetings so
we can get up
to speed on
current events.

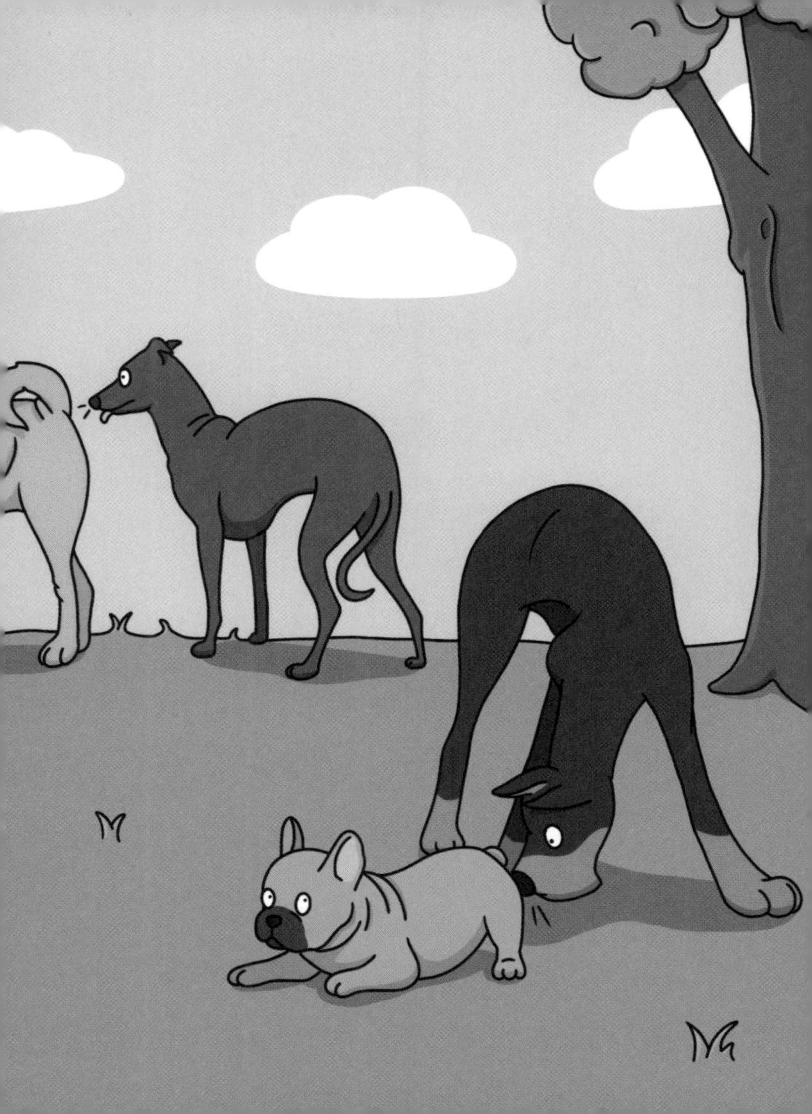

They don't let the cold stop us from going for our walkies!

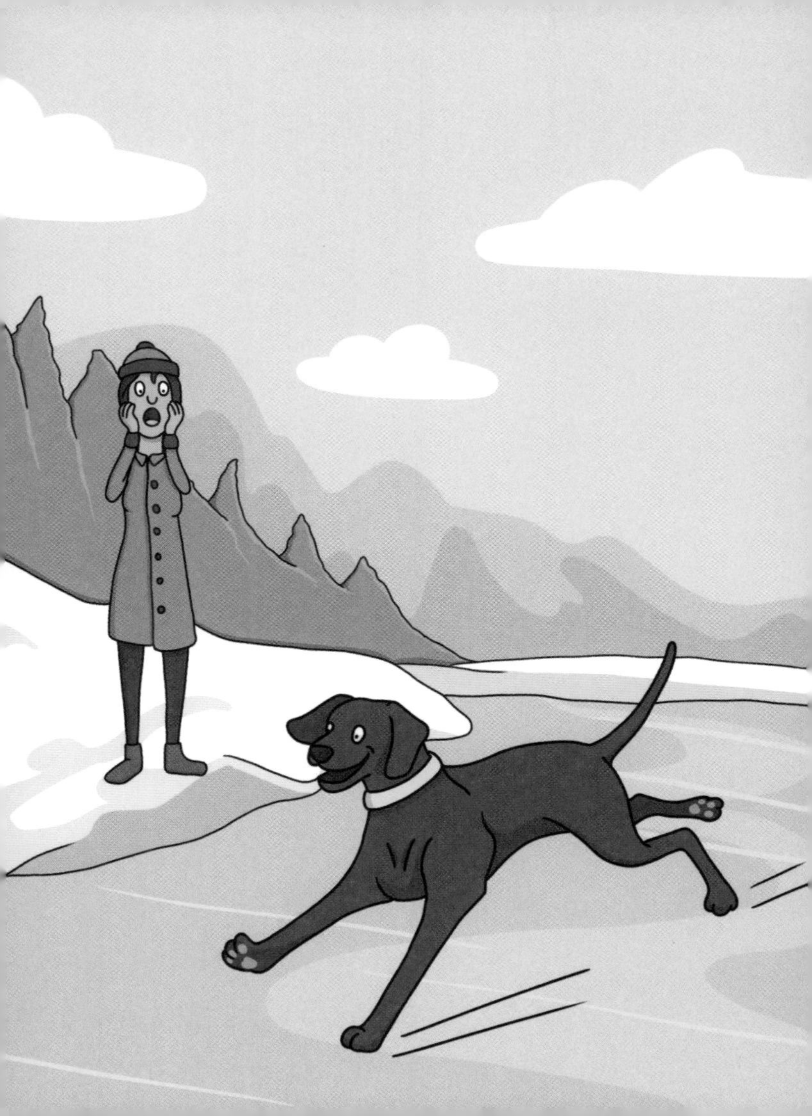

Our owners
help us out with
free childcare!

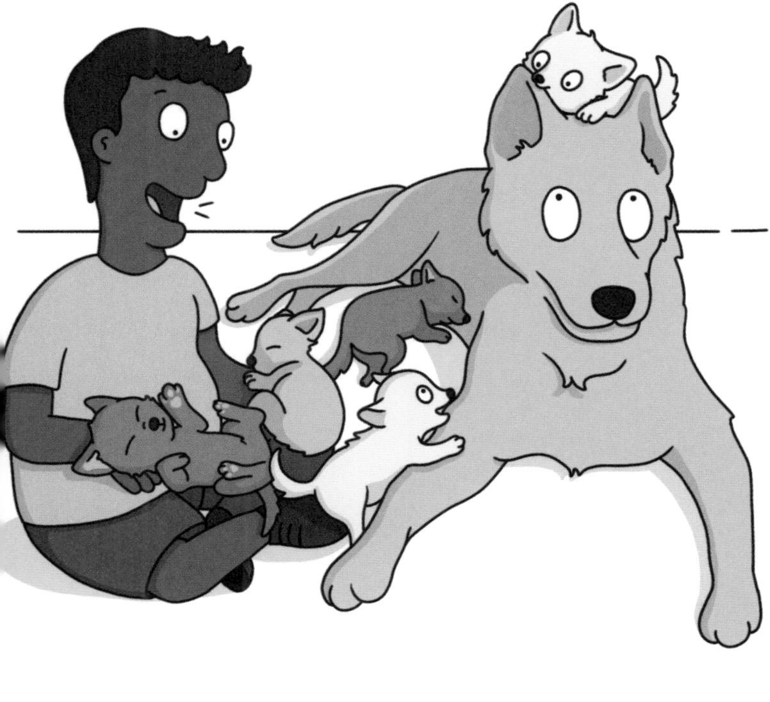

And we're always
happy to return
the favour!

They include us
in all their special
moments.

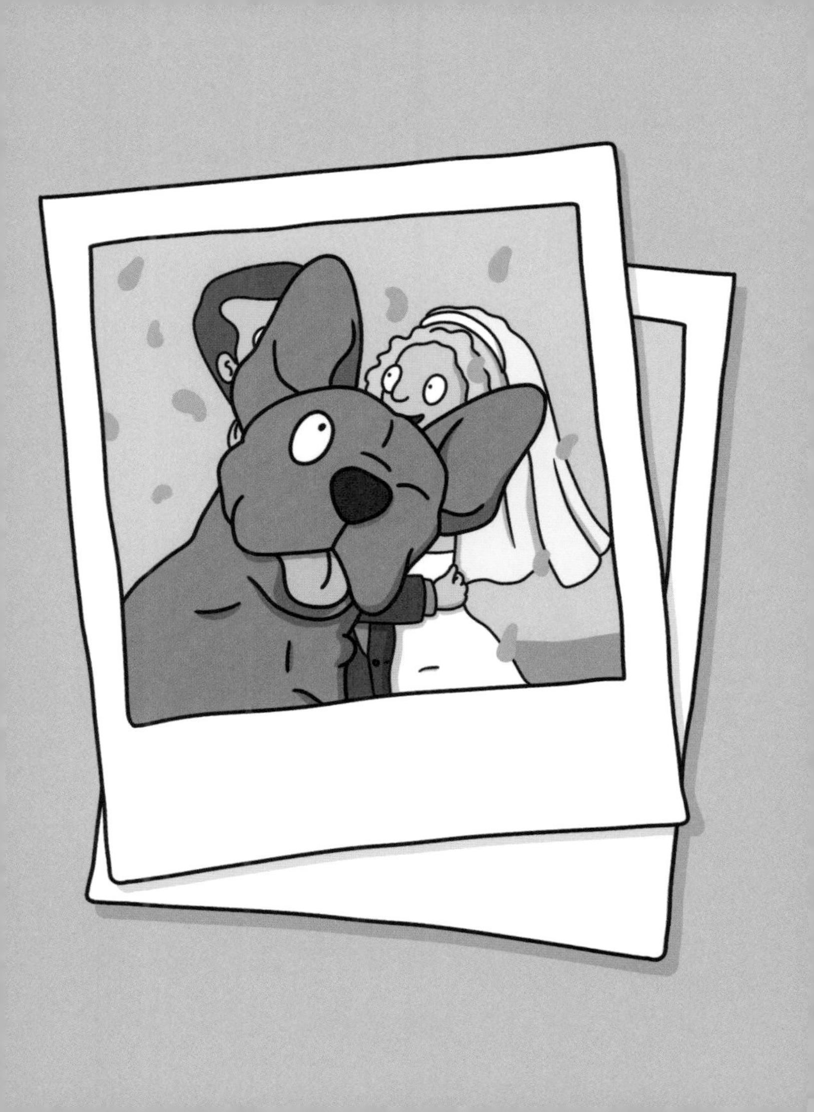

We love it when
they take us out
for a spa day!

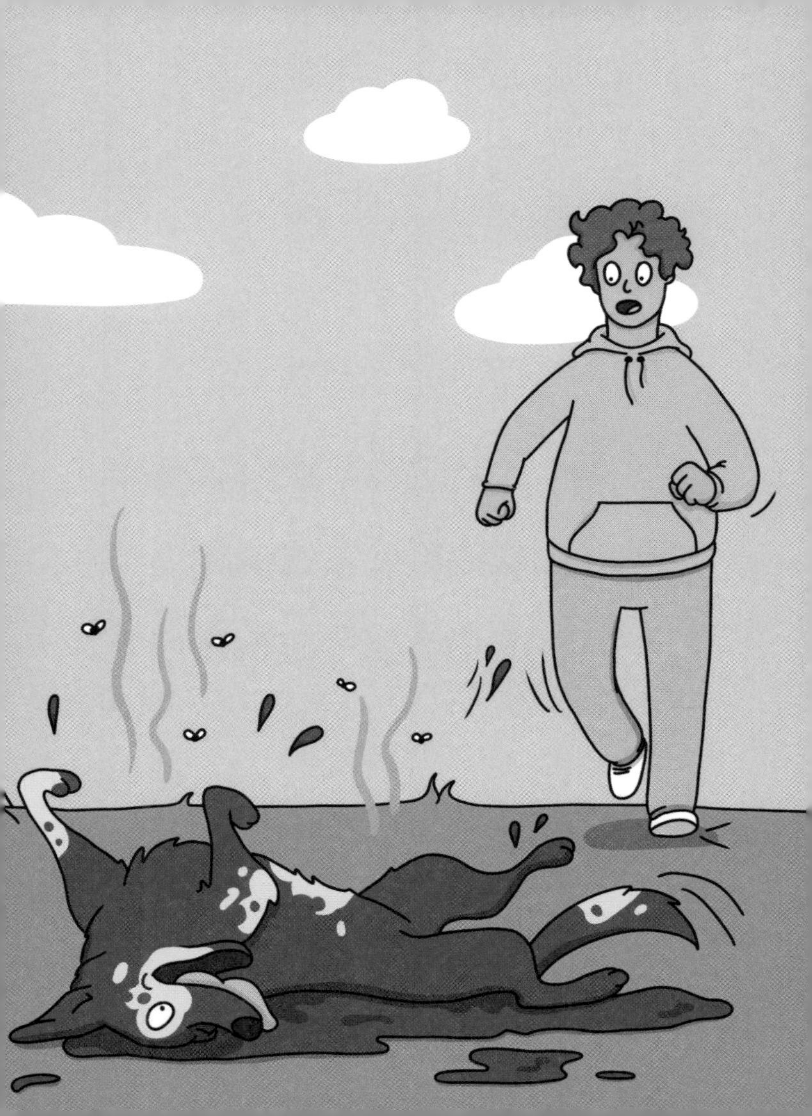

They teach us how
to make a good
first impression.

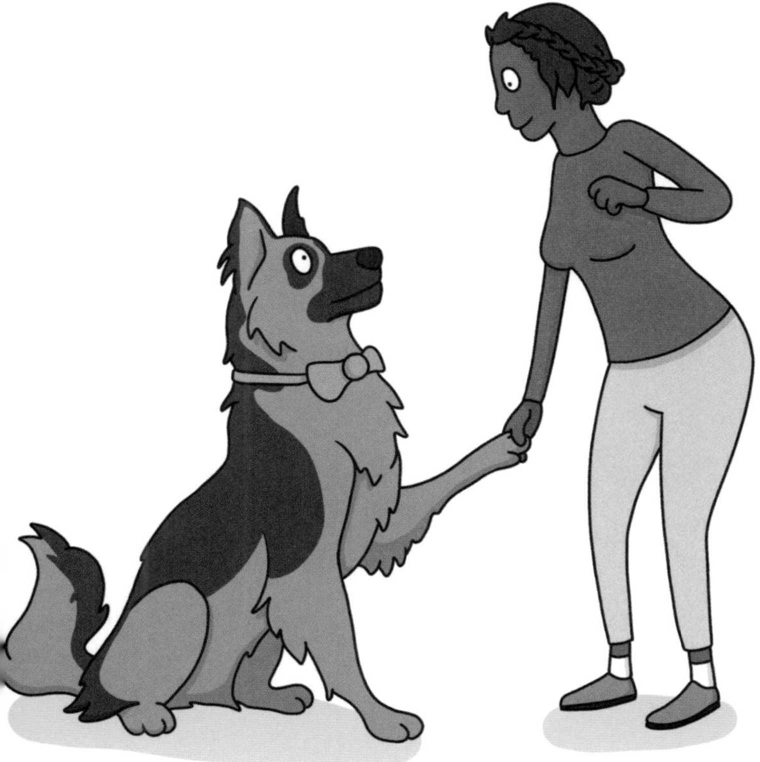

They support
our dreams!

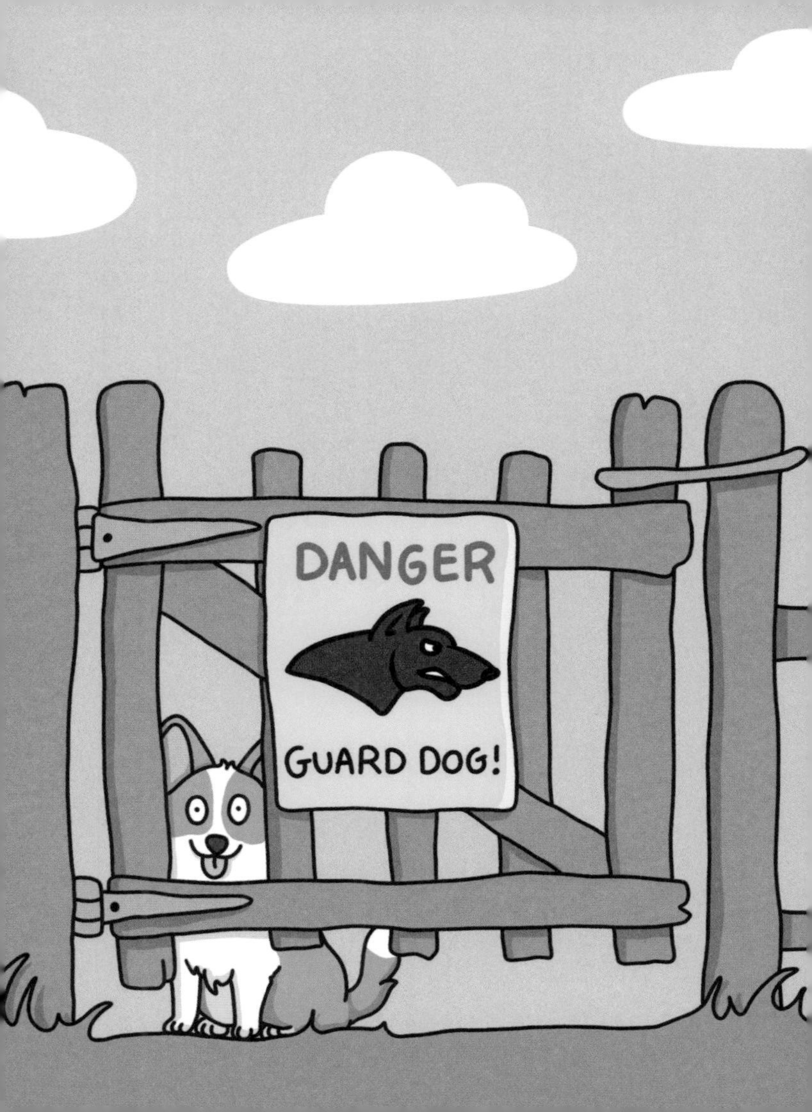
DANGER
GUARD DOG!

They give us our
own set of wheels!

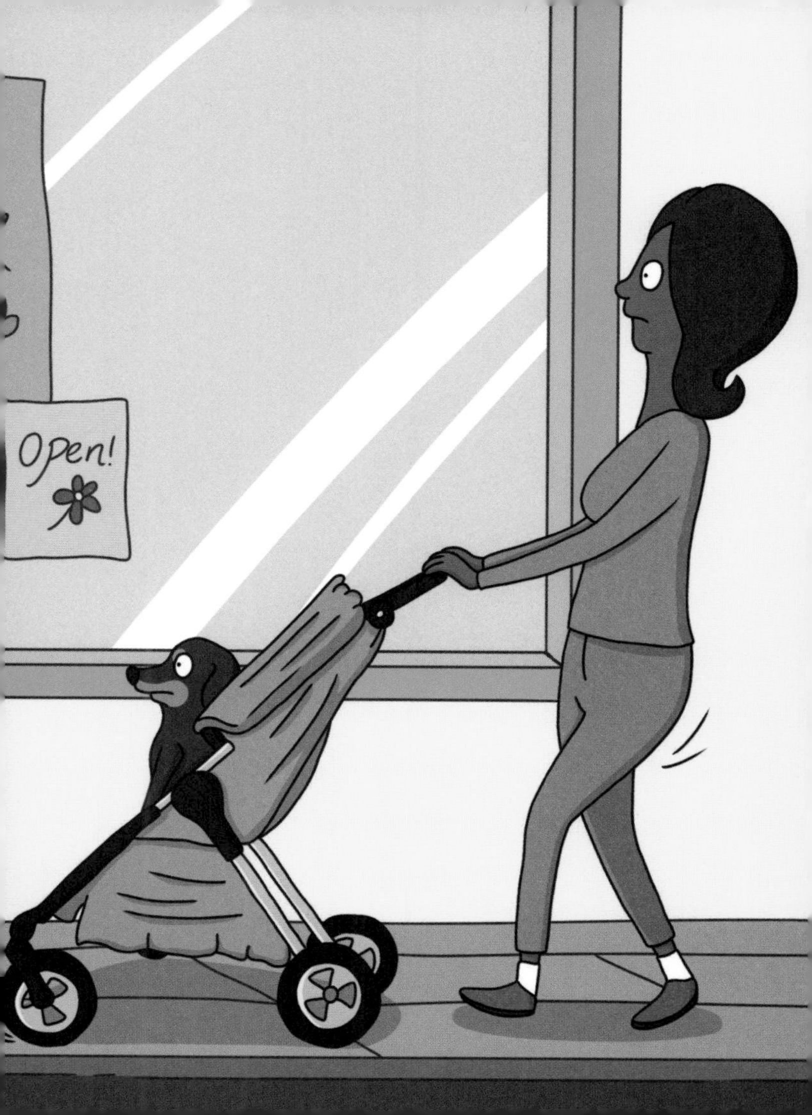
Open!

Our trips to the pool really make us feel alive.

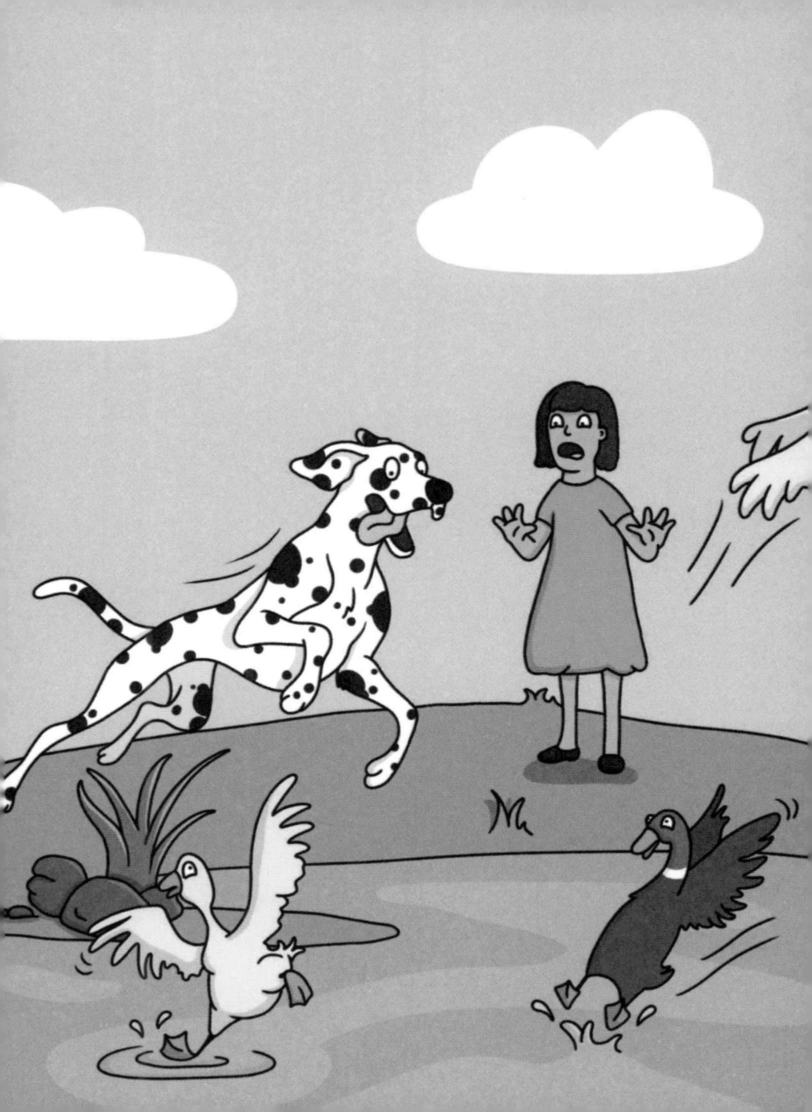

They recognize our rare and special gift for acrobatics.

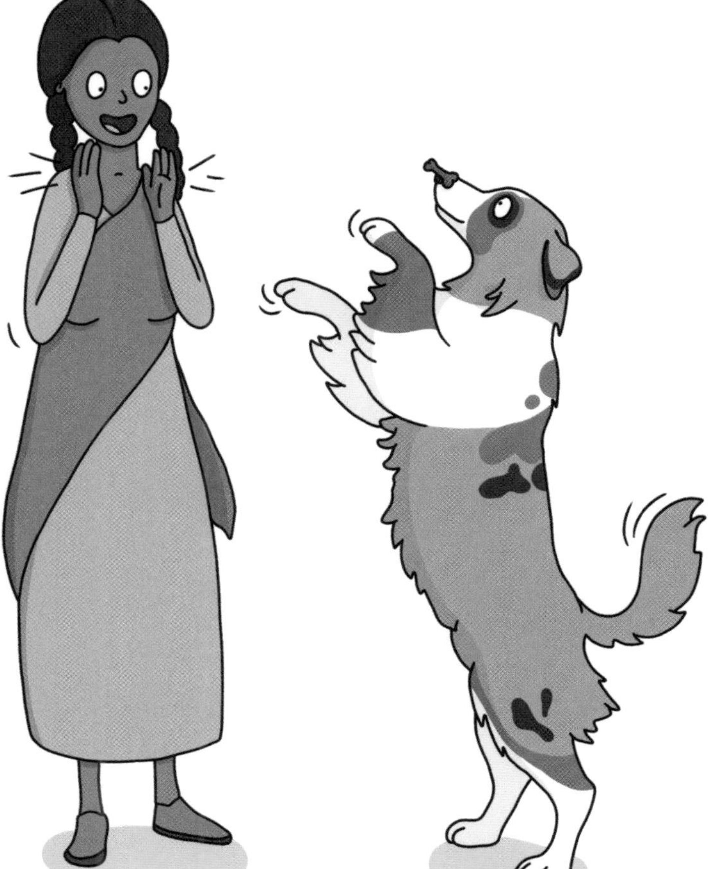

We are made
to feel like
important and
valued members
of the workforce.

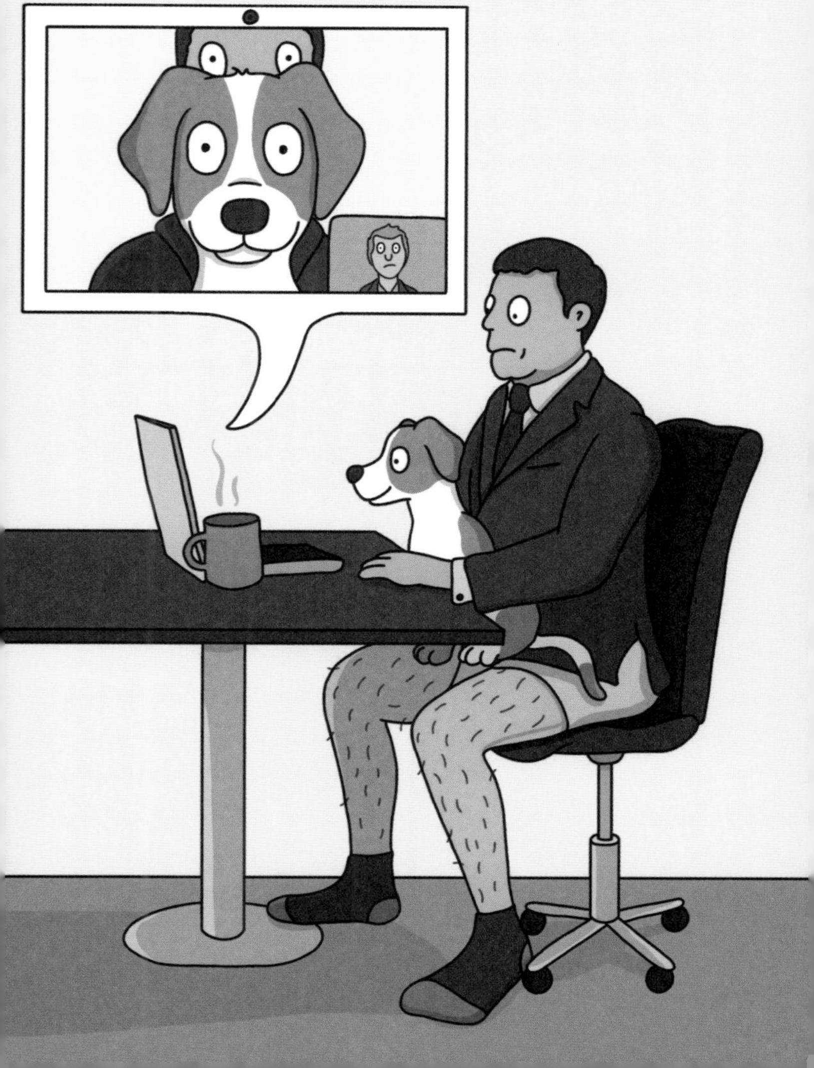

Humans make
sure our social
media presence is
always fabulous!

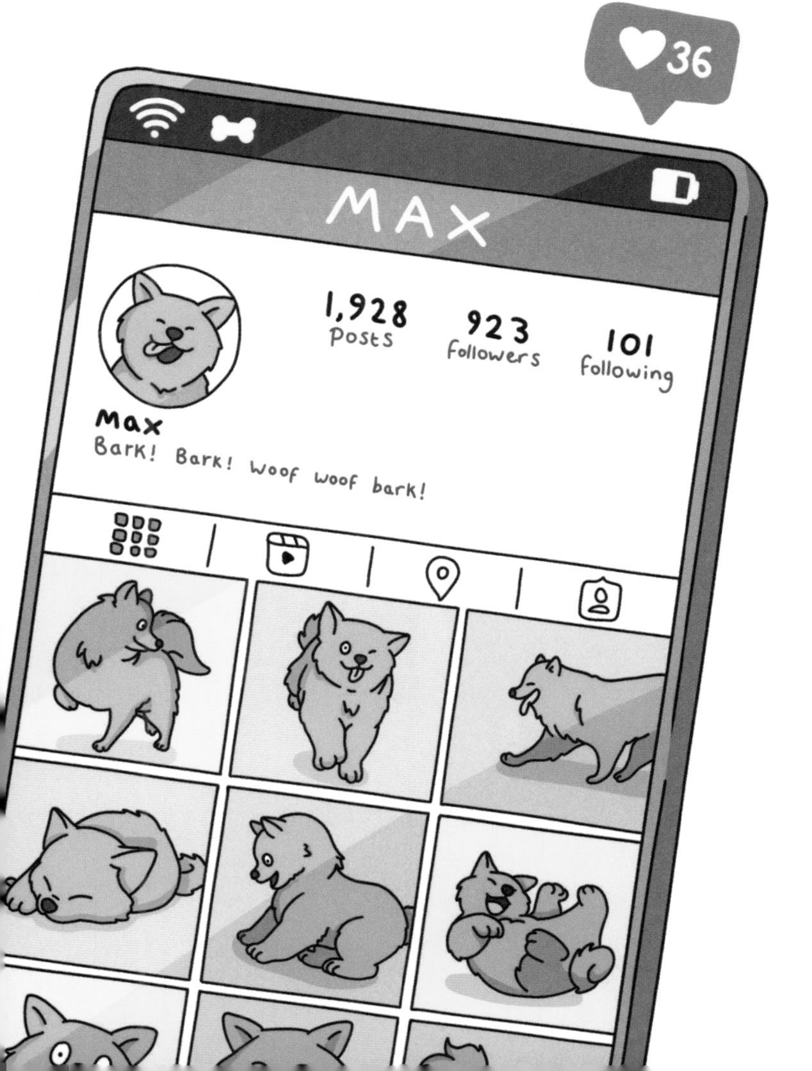
36
MAX
1,928
Posts
923
Followers
101
Following
Max
Bark! Bark! Woof woof bark!

But our favourite thing about them is that we get to see them every single day!

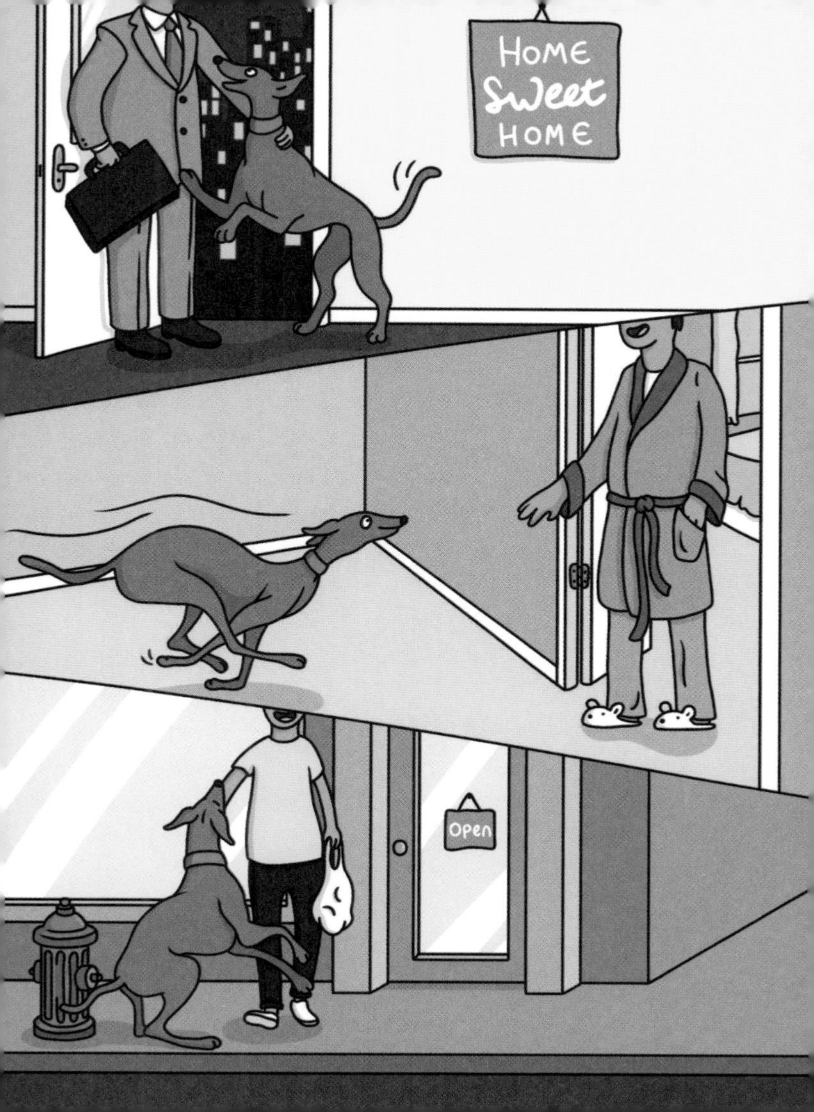
HOME Sweet HOME
Open

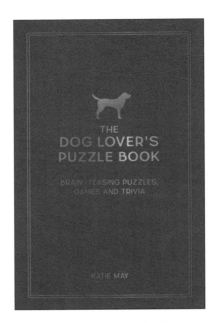

THE
**DOG LOVER'S
PUZZLE BOOK**

BRAIN-TEASING PUZZLES,
GAMES AND TRIVIA

KATIE MAY

978-1-80007-933-5
Hardback

When your hands need a break from giving nose-boops, or if it's raining cats and dogs outside, why not press "paws" and enjoy a puzzle or two? From classic conundrums and quizzes to crosswords and sudoku, whether you choose to while away the hours or dip a paw in, there's plenty within these pages to keep your mind as strong as a dog's devotion.

THE
DOG OWNER'S
SURVIVAL GUIDE

SOPHIE JOHNSON
ILLUSTRATED BY **TATIANA DAVIDOVA**

978-1-80007-400-2
Hardback

A hilarious, fully illustrated book of tongue-in-cheek advice for surviving life as a dog parent – the perfect gift for any dog lover. Containing all the tricks you need to help you navigate life with your furry friend, so you can focus on the positives, like giving them head-scritches and nose-boops whenever they prove they're a good doggo.

Have you enjoyed this book? If so, find us on
Facebook at Summersdale Publishers, on
Twitter at @Summersdale and on Instagram
and TikTok at @summersdalebooks and get
in touch. We'd love to hear from you!

www.summersdale.com

WHY YOUR DOG THINKS YOU'RE A HERO

Copyright © Summersdale Publishers Ltd, 2023

Text by Clare Wellham
Illustrations by Fin Kendall

An Hachette UK Company
www.hachette.co.uk

Summersdale Publishers Ltd
Part of Octopus Publishing Group Limited
Carmelite House
50 Victoria Embankment
LONDON
EC4Y 0DZ
UK

www.summersdale.com

Printed and bound in Poland

ISBN: 978-1-80007-931-1

Substantial discounts on bulk quantities of Summersdale books are available to
corporations, professional associations and other organizations. For details contact
general enquiries: telephone: +44 (0) 1243 771107 or email: enquiries@summersdale.com.